M000077265

The Lean Career

Start, Advance, or Change Your Career in the Modern World

Troy Buckholdt

Copyright © 2019 Troy Buckholdt

All rights reserved. No part of this book may
be reproduced or used in any manner without written
permission of the copyright owner except with the use of
quotations in a review.

First paperback edition October 2019

ISBN: 978-1-6915-5582-6

Contents

Preface

Are you confused about what to do after high school? Are you uncertain about what to do with your life? Many people who recently graduated high school or are not enjoying their current job are confused about what they should do. They don't know what to do with their life and many aimlessly just go to college as a default.

I have created a new model that will get you on a path to start a career you love. You will no longer think you are just drifting through life without a purpose. You will no longer waste tens of thousands of dollars on useless education. The process I've created is called *The Lean Career*. It is formulated with many of the same ideas taught by Eric Ries in his book *The Lean Startup*, which is responsible for the creation of many of the large tech companies you know today. *The Lean Career* also uses the same principles created by Toyota for reducing waste. You probably think that starting a career takes four years or more; yet through the elimination of waste, that time can be reduced to just months. I'm sure you also think you need to spend vast amounts of money on education to start a great career, yet through the use of technology, you can reduce that cost by over 100 times.

Have you heard people say that college isn't worth it or that you shouldn't go, but offer no good alternatives? This book shows you an alternative. You will learn exactly what you need to do to start a successful career without going to college. You will learn why people currently use the college model, it's inherent inefficiencies, and how to use a much more efficient model built for today's economy. If you implement the ideas taught in this book, within six months you could very well be on a great career path making over $50,000 a year.

Introduction

John Doe will serve as a fictional character of your typical student. All of John's life, he has been told that he will be going to college and that he needs to do well in school so he can get into a good college. He started his freshman year of high school with a 3.5 GPA. He joined three different clubs and started taking AP classes his sophomore year because he was told if he puts them on his college applications, it would help him get in. John doesn't really know what he wants to do in life but knows he will be going to college since he has been working towards college for as long as he can remember. He thinks that everything will be alright once he gets accepted into a good school.

John pushes through high school and finishes with a little over a 3.0 GPA and applies to four different state colleges. He feels really lucky that he got accepted to a local school and gets in-state tuition. John still doesn't know what he wants to do but thinks he will just figure it out during his first two years of college. After the first two years, John starts to worry about the student loan debt he is racking up but thinks he will get a good job and pay it off. It is also time for John to choose his major and he still doesn't really know what to pick, so he just chooses business since he was told that you could do anything with a business degree. John is excited to finally start learning something useful from his business classes and thinks he will learn everything required to get a great job. He learns about basic accounting, marketing, finance, and management. He feels like he is learning so much and even finds a sales internship over the summer.

After John graduated, he begins looking for a job and wants to find a role where he can apply the skills he learned in college. He thinks working in management would be cool, so he looks for management positions, but quickly realizes that they all want relevant work experience. He then thinks that maybe he can work in marketing or finance, but all the jobs want specific skills that he doesn't have. John begins to stress about just getting any job now that his $35,000 loan is racking up interest. John applies to every job that says entry-level or recent grads welcome. He gets a couple of interviews and realizes that all these jobs are basic sales positions with lower than expected pay. He takes the job to help start paying off his debt and moves back in with his parents. He plans on finding a better paying job later and then moving out of his parent's house.

After several years, John still had not found a better job and was working at the same company, slowly paying off his student loans without being able to save any money for a family or vacation. Statistically, this is the most probable outcome for the majority of people who attend college. This same story is told over and over again by so many recent graduates whose expectations weren't aligned with reality. They were led to believe that doing everything "right" would lead them to success. Don't be naive and follow in John's footsteps thinking this won't be you.

My Story

Here is a little background on myself, so you will understand why I am so passionate about the topic of starting a career using non-traditional education, aka not using the college model.

In high school, I chose the Math and Science Pathway, which required taking the hardest classes offered and would put me on track to becoming an engineer. At the start, I struggled in these classes but met someone who regularly slept during class yet got perfect scores on every test. He told me he had learned everything online during the summer. This really piqued my interest, and I began using different online resources like Khan Academy to do most of my learning for the tests. I figured out that I learned much better from online videos and was able to quickly research any topic I wanted to learn. This new way of learning helped me rise to the top of my class during freshman year with ease. However, I didn't think what I was learning would be useful to me, and I would often question the teachers about how I would use this in the real world. Their answers were always the same, "you need it to get into college."

This made me question college. I started reading story after story on Reddit of people who graduated from college but now worked in jobs like retail with over $30,000 in student loans. Once all the cost, debt, and time are added up, then it looks like a bad investment for what most people get out of it. It seemed like the more I learned about college, the more confident I became that I would be better off without it. This led me to start exploring different alternatives, and I began dabbling in welding, real estate, and sales during high school. I was able to apply my online learning techniques to succeed in all my endeavors. This was when I began questioning why ordinary people couldn't start their professional careers using online education instead of college since most white-collar jobs could be better learned online at a fraction of the cost.

After graduating from high school, the only thing on my mind was solving this problem by finding a way to allow people to start careers using online education. I knew that technology would play a massive part in the solution, so I started going to every tech meetup I could find in Atlanta. After attending a handful of these events, I quickly learned I was pretty useless without any specific business skills. I talked to the CEO of a billion-dollar startup in Atlanta at one of the events, and he confirmed that sales and product development skills are the most important attributes for building a startup. He also said it's extremely tough to be great at both, so it is better to become the best you can be in one and find a partner to do the other. At that moment, I doubled down and committed to start a successful sales career in technology, which would allow me to acquire the necessary skills to solve this education problem. I started researching all the different sales roles in technology and learned that the most common one was Sales Development, a recently formed position that only got popular in the last several years. Traditionally, a business to business technology salesperson would do the entire sales process. That includes everything from identifying the right companies to target, the correct people at the companies to set up meetings with, and ultimately closing the deal.

Just recently, executives discovered they could improve the efficiency of their sales process by splitting it up into different stages and assigning specialists for each stage. The first specialist in this process is the sales development representative. They are in charge of identifying the right companies and reaching out to the decision-makers at these companies through any means necessary to see if they would benefit from the representative's technology. They then schedule a meeting with the decision-maker that gets passed off to a more senior specialist called an account executive who is responsible for running the meeting and taking the deal to a close. This sales development role became very popular and in high demand with many companies. This caused the pay for this type of position to increase even though it was considered an entry-level role. I became extremely clear that my next move in life would be to get a position as a sales development representative to learn sales and how to build a technology company.

Since I was clear on what I wanted, I decided to work backward to figure out the best way to break into this role. I started looking at every job description for sales development representatives to figure out what it takes to get the job. I found that every job description was nearly identical. They all wanted excellent writing skills, great communication skills, and a 4-year degree. Most companies hired recent graduates with minimum sales experience while some wanted people with at least one year of relevant sales experience. It also didn't matter what degree you had or where it was from just as long as you had one. I questioned why they required a degree since it had no relevance to the job, so I started researching everything about it. I came to a firm conclusion that for the majority of companies it was only there to weed out people since it was an entry-level position that required almost no hard skills (hard skills are skills that can easily be identified on a resume). The lack of hard skills made it very difficult for recruiters to determine who is qualified, so they go with the assumption that people with a degree have better writing skills, communication skills, and business acumen.

The people they interviewed were likely to have just graduated from college with an unrelated degree and applied to this position only because of its minimum requirements. This meant that most of the people they interviewed had very little if no specific knowledge about what the job entails or how to be successful in it. I thought that I had at least the same level of communication skills as those recent graduates and they didn't have any distinct advantage over me other than having a piece of paper that made it easier for them to get an interview. This was when I came up with the hypothesis that if I could learn all about this one particular role and could do it effectively, then the decision-maker would have no choice but to hire me over the recent graduates.

I began learning everything about sales development and found some great resources, such as books, online courses, blogs, YouTube videos, etc. I was completely obsessed and spent over 12 hours a day submerged in the material. I quickly learned all the basics of business to business sales, along with even some of the more advanced techniques for the role. It took me about one month from when I started learning until I felt very confident in my ability to get a job. The next thing I did was to create a profile where I could outline all the resources I used to educate myself to prove I was competent. This profile page would show companies that I was very interested in the sales development position and learned from some of the smartest people in the industry. I then planned to use my newfound sales skills to reach out directly to the decision-makers in charge of hiring new sales development representatives at companies. This would allow me to skip the human resources team who would normally overlook any application or resume that didn't have a degree.

I had gone to a local entrepreneur meeting a day before I was going to reach out to companies, and I met the owner of a small technology company who was looking to hire a sales development representative. After showing him my education profile and my passion for the role, he offered me the position. While I was working at this company, I was able to use all the sales knowledge I recently acquired, and I was even able to learn about the inner workings of building a technology company due to its smaller size. I even got promoted to the more senior account executive position and was in charge of closing large six-figure enterprise deals along with managing another sales rep. At 18 years old, I was able to afford to move out and live in a nice apartment in Buckhead, one of the best areas of Atlanta. After work, I spent much of my time trying to figure out how others could use self-education to start their career as I did. As time went on, I began to feel like it was my responsibility to solve this problem, which could have a huge impact on the quality of life for millions of people.

While working, I was able to make a few savvy investments and build a credit score of nearly 800. After being at this company for about a year and a half, I saved up over $35,000 while supporting myself. I did things like surprising my parents with a one-week all-inclusive cruise to the Bahamas for my mother's birthday and going to fancy sushi buffets every couple weeks. I also decided it was time to start my own company to solve this education problem. I comfortably resigned from my job due to my savings and not having any debt. Before starting my company, I decided to take a few months to travel to places like Thailand, Costa Rica, and even take my girlfriend to Peru. I felt pretty lucky as a 19-year-old to be able to afford many of the luxuries of life. Working at a young age to save money while not having any debt really creates an optimal environment for opportunity.

Once I returned from traveling, I founded CourseCareers as my means to be able to accomplish my goal of transforming the way people start careers. I began spending all my time talking to students in high schools and universities to learn more about what they plan on doing, why they plan on doing it, and their expectations once they finish school. I also talked to recent graduates about their experiences with college and if their jobs aligned with their studies and matched their expectations. I even spoke with hiring managers at different

7

companies to learn what they were looking for. After analyzing all this information, I realized it was the entire model for traditionally starting a career that had enormous risks and inefficiencies. This was when I knew I had to create a new model for our untraditional economy. I developed CourseCareers as an online platform that assists people with every aspect of using this new model to help them start a career.

1

Why College?

Have you ever questioned why college exists in the first place? Why is it so big in the US when in other countries, apprenticeships and other forms of learning are still very prominent? In Switzerland, where college is free, over 70% of students still choose apprenticeships over college. In the US, over two-thirds of all high school students believe that college is the best option for them following high school. Over 70% of all recent high school graduates in the US enroll in college the following year. Over 80% of these recent high school graduates that enrolled as college freshman say that they are in college to start a career, yet only 27% of recent college graduates actually get a job in their field of study.

The best way to understand why we are currently in this college culture is to look back on the history of college in the US. This history will be split between pre 1944 and post 1944 due to a significant turning event.

Pre 1944 College History

In 1636, Harvard University was founded. It was the first university in the colonies before there was the United States. One of the primary purposes of the university was to train clergymen to go into the Ministry. The curriculum was mostly composed of the classical liberal arts to create well-rounded individuals. Between the 1600-1700s, the tuition for college was very affordable for most at a price of around one pair of shoes. There still weren't many people that went to college as most families needed their men to be working and couldn't afford to lose them to studies. The type of families that sent their kids to the university were often the wealthy ones that wanted the prestige and status that came along with it. Throughout this time, college was not a prerequisite to practice professions, and it was never about getting a job afterward.

In the 1800s, about 90% of all people lived on farms. The majority of lawyers and doctors didn't attend college but instead learned through apprenticeships. By the 1850s there were only a minimal number of business courses at colleges. The majority of people working in business learned through on the job training or sometimes a short multi-week course in a specific business discipline. Less than 20% of the people going to college studied a form of business compared to it now being, by far, the most popular.

From the 1850s - 1900s, the US began to enter the industrial age, and capitalism became popular. Many of the principles used for building our economy stemmed from the book *The Wealth of Nations* written by Adam Smith in 1776. It talks about how, through the use of specialization, we can improve efficiency and trade to create wealth for everyone involved. This trade and specialization are what led us to the industrial age, where people began specializing in disciplines such as farming, lumber, and building. People learned that these newly created professions for the industrial age had specific educational needs. This led more colleges to start training people in more practical professions such as machinists, farmers, and engineers.

During the 1900-1920s, only about 5% of recent high school graduates went to college as most professions still didn't require it. The biggest challenge for college administrators at that time was to try to convince people that they needed to go to college. For the students that did go to college, as many as 90% of them finished their studies after just two years. That time period also created many wealthy people who gave significant amounts of money to universities, which helped change the operation of colleges to run more similar to that of a business. This new wealth gave universities the ability to invest in fantastic architecture and sports teams to try to attract more students. During that same time, the college board was created to form standard entrance requirements such as the SAT.

From 1920-1944, the government was giving money to colleges for having a student army training program, now known as ROTC. More and more money was also given to colleges by wealthy individuals. All this new money led to even more campus architecture and sports teams. These advanced campuses and the growth of college sports in the US became a huge attractant for young people. This led to about 15% of all recent high school graduates attending college. The average tuition by the 1940s for private schools would be under $3000 in today's dollars, and public schools were much cheaper or even free. There still wasn't much value of having a college degree for the job market since most occupations didn't require academics. The majority of the value came from the network of the alumnus of the school. For example, if someone wanted to become a nurse, they would work in a hospital for free as an apprentice to learn and get their nursing diploma. This was great for the hospital as they got a significant source of free labor and great for people who wanted to become nurses.

Post 1944 College History

In 1944, we were fighting in WWII, and college played its part in helping the war efforts. Many of the research facilities in colleges helped advance military technology, which led to the government giving out many college grants. The other significant thing that happened in 1944 that forever changed college was the passing of the GI Bill. This bill allowed WWII vets to get free tuition at universities to help get them back into normal society. This led to colleges running large marketing programs toward vets since they knew it was an easy sell and they would get paid by the government. Within just a few years after passing this bill, colleges saw a 200-300% increase in enrollment.

In the 1950s-1960s, the government continued to give more money to universities to help with space research. This allowed universities to continue upgrading their facilities and sports teams to attract even more students. The government also started the federal student loan program, which allowed nearly anyone to get a loan for school. Imagine college being marketed as the coolest thing ever with your favorite sports team and now everyone has the choice between having fun at college or working in a boring job. As you can imagine, the number of recent high school graduates who began choosing college over work quickly grew. More universities lobbying in the government led to more careers, such as nursing, being regulated to require degrees to practice them. This gave universities large amounts of power through government force since going to college wasn't optional for many professions anymore.

If you have ever wondered why community college gets a bad rep, it's because of the GI Bill. This reputation started back in the mid-60s when so many vets applied to colleges, and the colleges had more applications than they could accept. The vets that didn't get accepted would often start in a community college and were looked upon as inferior since they were denied admission to a 4-year college. However, these same students would then transfer to a 4-year college afterward and often did better than the traditional students.

In the 1970s the government decided to change the subsidies they were giving directly to the university and instead give them to students in the form of need-based Pell grants. This raised tuition prices for the majority of students. There were about $10 billion in student loans in 1980 compared to the $1.5 trillion now. That is a 150 times increase. Throughout this time and the 80s, companies were also willing to invest in on the job training as they were only looking for candidates that had basic skills such as critical thinking, problem-solving, etc.

From the 1980s until now, tuition prices have consistently outpaced inflation by over 300%. The number of recent high school graduates enrolled in college has also continued to increase since colleges realized that higher prices didn't mean less enrollment because students can just borrow more. This has caused colleges to focus most of their efforts on continuously having the best campus and sports team to attract more students who are willing to pay the higher tuition.

Feeling Lucky? You've Been Indoctrinated

What is indoctrination? The definition is "The process of teaching a person or group to accept a set of beliefs uncritically." Have you or others you know accepted the belief that going to college is the best option and don't think critically about going? Even though this is one of the most significant life decisions for most people, they still don't think critically about it because they have been indoctrinated. This indoctrination has happened over people's entire lives, yet many don't even realize it.

When someone is indoctrinated, they believe something so strongly and aren't willing to question it, which also means they are willing to pay just about anything for it. This is why in the 1980s there was something called the Mt. Holyoke Phenomenon. This phenomenon was the idea that higher-priced tuition meant a more prestigious degree. Colleges learned that charging higher tuition increased not only the number of applicants but also the amount of higher quality ones too. (College indoctrination = degree at any cost)

This indoctrination has also been amplified by basic psychology. People want what they can't have. This is why even though colleges are charging huge amounts of money for tuition, students applying feel lucky when they get a chance to pay it (acceptance). This vast number of applicants applying to college is what allows colleges to play these mind games by making people feel privileged or lucky to get in. In what other industry would people be willing to pay money to apply to something (application fee) and pay even more money to go to their sales pitch on why you should buy it (orientation fee)?

Political Motives and Corruption

Most people don't realize that college is an enormous business. People make big dollars from universities, and some are even publicly traded with the goal of maximizing profit. Colleges can be split up into three types.

The first type of college is public, non-profit. These universities are the big state schools with huge campuses and sports teams that the majority of people attend because they can get in-state tuition. Some examples would be UGA,

Clemson, UCLA, etc. These schools are often heavily funded by the state and federal government. As much as 50% of their revenue comes from the government and is often tied to the student. For example, if a student enrolls in a public university and pays $20,000 a year, then the government is probably paying another $20,000 to the school. This makes the student worth $40,000 a year to the college. All this money that they make is then used to pay for the school's operation and expansions to attract even more students. They invest in things such as building new gyms, food courts, and upgrading their sports teams.

What most people don't realize about these public universities is the enormous amount of money being made even though they are non-profit, government-funded organizations. For example, there are many presidents of these public universities that are getting paid in excess of one million dollars a year. The president of Louisville University, James Ramsey made nearly 4.3 million dollars in 2016.

The high pay for the officials of the colleges is only a tiny fraction of the money being made from these universities. Think about all the money that public universities pull in each year from the government, students, and alumni. This number can easily reach into the billions. All this revenue means they are also spending it too. Imagine all the business that this creates, such as the restaurants on campus, the sports stadiums, etc. Who do you think wins these multi-million-dollar contracts to build and maintain the restaurant or stadium?

Public universities have something called a board. This board includes a group of people who make all the major decisions for the university. These decisions include what new majors they should create to what new buildings they should build and who they should hire to do so. Do you think that there might be some special interest between who sits on the board and who gets part of the billions in revenue?

For example, at the time of writing this, the University of Virginia has 19 members on the board who make the decisions for the school. The Governor appointed 17 out of these 19 members. The other two are a faculty appointed member and a student appointed member. Out of the 17 appointed, there are five who don't even live in the state of Virginia. Of the 12 who do live in the state, 10 of them contributed to the governor's political party. One of these members on the University of Virginia's board is the CEO of Dominion Energy. He was appointed to be on the board in 2017. In 2018, The University of Virginia decided to buy the power generated by a planned 15-megawatt solar power array outside of Richmond under a new agreement with Dominion Virginia Power. This purchase will most likely profit Dominion in the millions.

After the decision to make this purchase, Colette Sheehy, the University's senior vice president for operations, said "We had confidence, however, that strategies and new technology would develop over time. The Hollyfield and Puller agreements with Dominion Energy represent a key strategy that will enable the University to meet the goal set by the board."

Who do you think helped influence "the goal set by the board?" I'm assuming the people on the board, like the CEO of Dominion, was able to influence that goal. One of the reasons people donate money to political campaigns is to get on these college boards. Now, do you understand all the corruption and special interest groups who make huge amounts of money from our student loan debt and taxes?

Since the governor is getting so many donations from special interest groups to be on the board of colleges, they have a strong interest in convincing everyone that they should go to college to continue this cycle of donations. The corporations benefiting from our student loans and taxes also have a very strong interest to keep people going to universities. This is one reason why politicians talk about how everyone needs to go to college.

The second type is private, non-profit. This type of university is very similar to public ones, except they don't get money from the government. These colleges often cost more since they are not government funded like other public schools. This is why these schools do not have in-state tuition. Some examples include Harvard, Stanford, New York University, etc. These schools operate very similarly to public schools since they are also non-profit. The presidents of these schools often also get paid in the millions. They also have their board, which makes decisions on how the college should spend their money. This is where, just like public universities, the corruption and special interest groups come into play, allowing for many people to profit greatly.

The third type of college is private, for-profit. This is the last type of university and also the one that is run most like a business. The goal of a private for-profit university is to make a profit for their shareholders. Many times, these universities are considered diploma mills as the people that come out of them rarely learn anything and instead just have a piece of paper. Some examples of these types of schools include the University of Phoenix, Strayer University, etc. The CEO who runs Bridgepoint Education, the parent company of Ashford University, makes about $20 million a year. The CEO of Apollo Group, the parent company of the University of Phoenix makes about $11 million a year. All the money these universities make is distributed back to their shareholders that own the company. This means all federal grants and student loans go straight to helping make these individuals rich.

Many of the politicians have even more motive for you to go to college. The number of Democratic teachers outnumbers Republican teachers 12:1. This makes college teachings very liberal and after being submerged in it for 4-6 years, it very likely that the students will have a liberal view. This is why you will probably hear Obama or other Democrats strongly voicing how everyone should go to college.

Student loans are also a huge business. At $1.5 trillion dollars, there are a lot of businesses that get their share of the pie. One of the most prominent types of companies that benefit from student loans is the federal debt servicing companies. These are the companies that are in charge of collecting the money students owe from federal loans by all means necessary. This includes contacting the students, providing alternative payment options, and even garnishing wages. One of the biggest companies that does student loan servicing is Navient. It manages more than $310 billion dollars in student loans, and the company itself is worth over $2.8 billion dollars with more than 2,500 workers. Another big part of the student loan business is the private student loan. Wells Fargo and Sallie Mae are the biggest lenders out there with over $20 billion in loans. These companies have a very strong interest for people to continue going to college and racking up debt. It's likely they even put aside money to help market college to students or lobby in the government. It seems the only ones not benefiting are the students and taxpayers supporting these lies and corruption.

It Worked for Your Parents, Grandparents, and Teachers

I'm sure you've been told by your parents and grandparents your whole life that you need to go to college to be successful. They are probably telling you this because either they went to college and it worked for them, or they've been influenced by politics and college marketing to believe it's the best option for you. Back in the 1990s, when college was much less expensive, the debt could often be paid back relatively easy. It was also more valuable back then as not nearly as many people had a degree, so it helped differentiate people when looking for a job. Back then there also wasn't the internet, so the best way to learn was in college. Since college worked for your parents and grandparents, they strongly believe in its value and want to give you the same privilege they had. This makes them willing to push their kids to go and pay whatever it takes. The parents who didn't go to college probably saw their friends who did go become more successful than themselves, so they think that you shouldn't make the same mistake they did of not going to college.

Some parents actually use which college their kids go to as a bragging tool among other parents. This makes some parents just want their kids to go to the best college or the same college they went to so they can feel like they won the competition. I've seen these countless times as I've talked to parents who seem much more interested in talking about which college their kids got into rather than what they are learning or working on. For parents who don't have many of their own accomplishments, this becomes their most proud accomplishment too, which makes them push their kids to get into the best school even if it isn't the best option for their kids.

Another group of people who I'm sure have been telling you that you need to go to college ever since you were in kindergarten are your teachers. Since a college degree is a requirement to become a teacher, this makes your teachers inherently biased towards having a degree. Also, to move up in the ranks as a teacher, you need to go back to school to get a better degree. This has caused teachers to think of degrees as one of the most essential things in life. Teachers also work for the government and are heavily influenced by the politicians who try to push college on everyone.

Since both family and teachers have been telling their kids that they're going to college, this has put students on a tracked path. They are working backward from this goal of going to college instead of the real goal of starting a great career that they can love and support themselves with. This tracked path often blinds students from thinking anything past college and only allows them to think one step at a time towards reaching this goal of college. This is why students have such a hard time questioning going to college. It's because there are guard rails on each side of them and seemingly every action they take, points straight toward reaching this goal of attending college. Every good grade and class in middle school is to get into high school. Every good grade or advanced class in high school is to get into a good college. If you do well in high school, then you are by default preparing to go to college.

Fear Sells

There are many students who don't actually want to go to college or think the cost isn't worth it. These same students will still go because both they and their parents are afraid of what will happen if they don't go. This is because colleges have learned that the best emotion to cater to is fear. Colleges have

Why College?

invested heavily in making people think that college is the only option, and without it, you can only work in a job flipping burgers. The infamous billionaire Peter Thiel often refers to college as being either one of three things.

- An investment product
- A consumption good
- An insurance policy

He thinks that it is most likely an insurance policy for the majority of people. This became very apparent to me as I talked to many students currently enrolled in college who have entirely different plans with their life after they graduate. Some that I've spoken to just want to work odd jobs and travel. Others want to start a business or work in an industry completely unrelated to their major. I often ask them why they are going to college and spending all this money if they want to do something completely different. Their answer usually is something to the tune of "I want to have something to fall back on" or "I want to first get my diploma to be safe." These students have been taught to fear the unknown of not going to college and think that this college insurance will save them if their real plan doesn't work out.

Thiel also likes comparing the similarities between college and the Catholic church 500 years ago. He talks about how people think that if they get into the right college, they will be saved, but if they don't, they will be in trouble. This is the same way the Catholic church sold indulgences 500 hundred years ago through catering to people's fear that if they didn't buy them, then they would go to hell. If you get a diploma, you're saved; otherwise, you are a failure. College has convinced people, just like the church did, that the only way to get saved in our society is by getting a diploma through college. Colleges also invest heavily in marketing this fear to you. This becomes very apparent if you google anything questioning if college is the right choice to only find many edu websites with articles scaring you of what will happen if you don't go rather than addressing real concerns.

Reality Sucks

Another big reason people go to college is to put off facing the real world. When an 18-year-old is given a choice to either work in a boring job or have fun at a university with their friends, the majority will choose the university. There are two main reasons for this.

The first reason is that this person doesn't want to face the real scary world by having to work at a job and make real money to pay real bills. They would much rather live inside their fake, safe environment in college where you don't need to have a job to get fake money (Student Loans) to pay your college dues. I've personally witnessed this time and time again as students graduate college without any knowledge of the real world and can't find a job. Instead of coming to the realization of their situation and dealing with it, they instead, decide to go back to school for a master's degree to delay facing the real world for another two years.

The second reason is for the social environment. It is much more exciting to party in college with your friends than it is to work in a tedious job. I'm sure you've also heard of people saying that college is a good way to test what the real world is like in a safe environment. This is a big lie as college is not the real world, nor is it anything like it. It's simply extended adolescence. The only way to experience the real world is by living in the real world.

Everything Is Better on the Other Side of the Rainbow

Have you ever heard some of your extended family or friends tell you the reason they aren't successful is because they didn't go to college? The reason people often say this is because they want to blame an external factor for their failures, and college is the most logical one. A common human trait is to think that everything is better on the other side of the rainbow. For example, people often think life would have been great if only they did XYZ or life will finally be great after they do XYZ. These people often put college on a pedestal and think that everything would have worked out if only they had gone to college when in reality, they would have been in the same spot whether they went to college or not.

People Don't like to Admit They Made a Bad Decision

There are many people who have graduated from college and now work in the job they could have easily gotten without going to college. These same people will say that their college degree was worth it because they grew a lot as a person while they were in college and learned about life. They could be $50k in debt and still say it was worth it. There are two main reasons for this. The first is that they cannot fathom to think that if they didn't go to college, then they would have still grown as a person and learned about life. The fact that they probably lived on their own for the first time, met new people, got a job, and did taxes all have nothing to do with growing as a person. They give all the credit to college, which in turn creates this artificial value.

23

This is like a doctor back in the 1400s that would crush up random plants, give it to a person with a cold and tell them it will make them better in 5-8 days. The person would have gotten better by default without their potion, but they instead give credit to the doctor who creates this artificial value.

The second reason is that people don't want to admit they made the wrong decision. People will often do whatever it takes to defend their decision, so they don't have to admit they were wrong. This can be so ingrained that it is even subconscious. This can go as far as to where they will tell others to make the same mistake they made, so they can feel better about their decision.

The Value You Get out of College

Most people associate college with education, but the education is actually only a very small piece of what students are buying. There are three parts to a traditional college: education, network, and experience. The education is what most people think you get from going to college. You get to learn new things and are supposedly "educated" afterward. This education could be on lower-level courses required during the first two years or upper-level courses in the following years. These studies usually consist of books, lectures, classroom discussions, and homework.

The education can be very important for some people who are studying an industry that is regulated to require a degree such as a doctor, lawyer, or engineer. In these cases, the education can very well be the most valuable part of going to college. For the majority of people who aren't studying these types of regulated fields, the education doesn't contain nearly as much value because education is like a commodity. You can

24

learn it virtually anywhere and in many ways. For example, if someone is a history major or psychology major, then they could easily read books for free to learn the same information they would have gotten in class. Only in rare cases where someone is at a top school with the top professors in the world, they can get a higher quality education from the professors' first-person experiences that can't be obtained elsewhere. Try to imagine how many people would go to college to study business if they were told they would not get a degree or internship and they had to live with their parents since the college didn't have any dorms, social life, or activities. That would be a pretty hard sell since it only contained the education. The key takeaway is that for most people the education usually is not that valuable or that big of a selling point.

The network consists of college alumni, classmates, and the brand of the college degree. This is normally the most valuable part people acquire from college to help start their career. This is also the reason you've probably heard more people use the phrase "getting a college degree" instead of "getting a college education." This college degree is only valuable because there is a network (group) of people who say it's valuable. There are multiple ways this network affects someone's ability to get a job.

The first reason the network of the college degree is valuable is because the vast majority of people in charge of recruiting and hiring for companies have college degrees. This makes them biased towards favoring people with degrees since they probably attribute their degree to opening up an opportunity or bettering themselves. This same principle can be attributed to nearly any positive similarities that the person in charge of recruiting has with the people applying. This could be anything from going to the same college to playing football or having both worked at McDonald's.

Another very important aspect of the college network is the work opportunities attached to being a college student. Nearly all internships are only associated with college students making it very difficult for anyone else to gain entry-level experience in an industry. This has become especially important in recent years since more and more companies are hiring permanent employees directly out of their internship programs.

The recruiting team also uses college degrees as a signal for choosing who to interview for a position. Not too long ago, having a college degree told company recruiters that you were smart, ambitious, and the top talent of society. Since then, having a college degree tells recruiters you probably have at least some intelligence and persistence to make it through four-plus years. The value of just having a degree has gone way down throughout the years as the requirements to get a degree have become much easier, and there has become a surplus of graduates. This small piece of value that comes along with just having a degree is usually the only value that private for-profit universities sell. Since the number of people going to college is so high, recruiters also assume that people who don't go to college must not be smart or motivated enough. I've personally witnessed this after attending multiple business meetings and having intelligent conversations with people. These individuals always assume I must have gone to college because they are shocked when they find out I never went. This is the reason you've probably heard people say that it doesn't matter what degree you have as long as you have one.

An even more important signal that comes along with having a college degree is where it is from, the major, and GPA. By far, the most important is where the degree is from. A degree from a low tier state school or for-profit online school in psychology might get you a job at Starbucks while the same psychology degree from Yale might get you a job at Goldman Sachs. This is because the value of the college degree comes from the exclusivity and reputation of the school who gave it out. This is why Ivy League schools, such as Harvard, only accepted 2,023 students in 2018 compared to 2,444 in 2006. With more and more people going to college and Harvard having more resources than ever with over $39 Billion in the bank, why don't they teach more students? The reason is the same as why a Studio 54 nightclub doesn't let in more people even if there is still room. It's because the value comes from the exclusivity, which in turn attracts the best people. Peter Thiel, who went to Stanford, often talks about how Ivy League schools don't create great business leaders or lawyers, but instead, they attract and identify the best people who are innately smarter and more motivated. Since companies trust that 2,023 students out of the 2,023 students accepted at Harvard are already the brightest people in the world, they will hire just about any one of them.

Schools also develop their own network of employers that actively hire out of their programs. For example, there is a college in Georgia that is one of the only schools having a logistics major. This major has attracted many logistics companies to hire people directly out of this college's program. Georgia Tech is a college known for having an excellent computer science program and attracts many high-tech companies that hire out of this program. Usually the more prestigious schools will have more and better companies hiring out of their programs while the lower tier state schools will have lower-tier companies. Some for-profit universities don't even have any network of employers at all.

The rest of the value of the network comes solely from the people at the school, including the alumni that graduated from the school and the other students who are studying at the school. Starting with the Alumni, the first reason they are important goes back to one of the earlier points I made about the bias recruiters have towards their similarities with the applicants. Since people normally take pride in which school they went to, this similarity becomes increasingly powerful for getting a job. This is also the reason it is so difficult for anyone who didn't go to a top school to work at the best companies on Wall Street or Silicon Valley. It's because many of the recruiters at these companies went to a top school and are bias towards hiring others from a top school. The second reason alumni are important is because they sometimes work closely with schools and teachers to actively help connect students to opportunities. Alumni understand the programs and often want to give back to help other students since they also went through the same experience.

Students you meet through college classes and associations can also be valuable because they could help you get a job at companies they work at in the future or even become partners in starting a business. The value of the students you network with are also in line with the quality of talent the school accepts. For a top school such as Stanford, other students you meet might already have companies worth millions of dollars or will be running billion-dollar companies in the future. The relationship with these types of students is much more valuable than the students you meet at a frat party in a lower-tier state school since they likely won't have the same connections. The key takeaway is that the network is usually the most valuable part as far as starting a career goes.

The experience is everything from living on your own, college activities, parties, food, travel, sports teams, relationships, etc. Everything that makes college seem cool or fun is part of the experience. While the experience has very little to do with starting a career, it is the biggest attractant schools use to bring in young people. For example, after the GI Bill got passed and a huge influx of men enrolled in college, it became apparent that women should go to college if they want to find a husband. This became so popular that it became known as the MRS Degree. This, in turn, also made more men want to go to college due to all the women. Another example could be the huge frat parties and drinking that goes on during college. Both of these are considered part of the college experience.

Most state colleges are focused on selling this experience to attract their students. I know of some lower-tier colleges that even have gourmet buffets and huge amazing architecture. You probably won't see too many state schools touting how much their students make on average or how little debt they have, but they will sell what life is like during college and how fun it is. Some schools are known for their amazing sports teams and games which they spend hundreds of millions of dollars on yearly. The majority of the tuition and fees will be spent on improving the experience to attract even more students. The huge increase in amenities is also part of the reason why colleges have had an explosion of administrators, which also contributes to the higher staff overhead.

One of my friends who goes to a state school in Georgia tells me how they have one of the best college buffets. He can get steak every day and sometimes even lobster for dinner. This is one of the biggest selling points for this college, and I'm sure you could imagine how this would attract someone to a school even if it doesn't have anything to do with the education or network. Think about it. Do you ever hear anyone talk about "college life" or brag about the parties and sports teams? If someone goes to college because of the experience, then it is not an investment product or insurance product. It is actually a consumption good.

Another part of the college experience that really attracts people is the party lifestyle. Think about the crazy college spring breaks or wild frat parties that happen. This party experience is so important to some young people that they make their decision on which college they attend almost solely based on it. In many of the other countries that have free college, such as Switzerland, the party scene isn't anything like the US. Perhaps many people in Switzerland choose apprenticeships over universities because the college experience isn't much different from the apprenticeship experience. While the party scene might be fun, it can very negatively affect people that might want to have a career once they graduate. This can be attributed to the addiction of drugs and spending time partying instead of learning and networking. The key takeaway is that the experience is the reason most young people want to go to college.

2

The Problems with Using College to Start a Career

If someone wants to go to college to just have a good time, that's completely fine. If someone wants to go to college to learn some interesting things, that's also completely fine. However, if someone wants to go to college to start a career, that's not such a good idea for most people. This is a big problem since more than 80% of freshmen said that the main reason they are in college is to get a good career.

The Huge Cost People Call an Investment

One of the biggest reasons college is a bad idea for most people is due to the enormous costs associated with it. Most people think the only cost associated with college is the tuition, but it is actually much more. The numbers below don't take into consideration taxes and are based on numbers, that from my experience, I believe are very probable.

The first part of the investment is the money college actually costs. This includes tuition, books, fees, housing, and ordinary living expenses. While the in-state tuition might not seem like that much, once all the costs are added up, the average total cost for one year at an in-state school comes to around $25,000. If a student were to graduate in 4 years at an in-state school, this makes the total cost $100,000. If someone were to go to a private university, then the average cost quickly exceeds $50,000 a year, making the total cost over $200,000 for someone who graduates in 4 years. Georgia has the HOPE scholarship, which pays for 90% of in-state tuition for those who have over a 3.0 GPA. This scholarship has made people think college is nearly free, but after they enroll in college and realize how quickly all the costs add up, they easily find themselves spending over $15,000 a year.

The second part of the investment is the opportunity cost of someone's time that could have been spent making money. The opportunity cost very quickly exceeds the money spent on college. I estimate that the average 18-year old who is smart enough to get into a good college could also use The Lean Career Model to make between $40,000-$60,000 a year during their first four years of work. This means that someone would be ahead $160,000 - $240,000 if they worked instead of going to college for four years. If it took someone six years to graduate, this total would be $240,000 - $360,000. If someone's evaluating the cost of college, then they also need to include this in their analysis.

The third part of the investment is the experience cost that someone would have spent being in a classroom instead of getting real-world experience and promotions. This is a very significant part of the cost that most people don't take into consideration. For many roles, someone with over four years of experience would be making double what a recent graduate without experience would. This could be due to their expertise in the role or the promotions they got at the company over the years. An example of this would be if both, the person with experience and the recent college graduate, are 22 years old, yet the person with experience makes $80,000/year while the recent graduate makes $40,000/year. Over the next several years, the person with experience would likely make in excess of $100,000 before the recent graduate catches up.

The last part of the investment is all the time and money someone spends in high school preparing for college. These costs include time and money spent doing well in high school, preparing for the ACT and SAT tests, taking these tests, applying to colleges, touring them, and going to orientation. All this time and money could have been spent preparing for a career using The Lean Career Model or working on a business. This is the reason you probably hear about people in their teens having multi-million-dollar companies or having a high profile career by the age of 20. One person who comes to mind is Matt Mickiewicz. At age 14, he spent his time working on building websites, and by age 16, he was skipping class to sell advertising deals on his website for tens of thousands of dollars. Since he focused on business instead of school and didn't go to college, by the time he was 30 he had founded three very successful companies with each doing millions in revenue and giving him a net worth of over 100 million dollars. Matt said, "Focusing on business as my goal early on is what put me on a path to building multiple companies. If my goal was college, I don't think I would be where I am today."

Another person that comes to mind is James Boehm. We both went to the same high school, and like Matt, he also focused on business instead of school. At age 14 he founded a company called MCProHosting which was doing millions in revenue before he even graduated high school making him one of the youngest millionaires. Instead of going to college, once he graduated, he founded a second company, Beam.io. At age 20, he sold it to Microsoft for an undisclosed amount. He currently holds a position as the Head of Community at

Microsoft. In both of these cases, the founders of these companies wouldn't have been able to do this if they focused all their attention on getting into a good college instead of working on their companies.

Student Loans Hurt

Debt…. This is something people know isn't good, yet they underestimate its significance. As of this writing, there are about 1.5 trillion dollars in student loan debt in the US. That is more debt than credit card debt. $1.5 trillion is 1 thousand 500 billion. To give you some reference to just how much money that is, the top 10 richest people in the world are worth 744 billion at the time of this writing. $1.5 trillion dollars is more money than 4 billion people in the world have combined and is over half of the world's population.

Here are the numbers. The average student loan debt per student is $35,000 as of this writing. The average interest on that debt is 5.8% paid over ten years. This means the monthly payment would be $385 and, if always paid on time, the total spent would be $46,200. That's an additional $11,000 in interest. Another very important thing to note is that student loan debt is the only type of debt that bankruptcy cannot be declared on, which makes it very dangerous. For all other types of debt, like getting a loan to buy a car or a house, the worst-case scenario is that you declare bankruptcy because you cannot afford it anymore and the debt disappears along with your credit score, but you can continue to live your life and rebuild. With a student loan, if you get hurt or can't pay for any reason, the interest will quickly build up. After just five years of no payments, a $35,000 loan at 5.8% interest would increase to over $46,000.

There is also no way to get out of not paying the loan back. The government has the right to automatically take the money out of someone's paycheck, tax refund, or social security. There is no way to stop them. This has caused many people with large student loans to just give up on trying to pay it off. They pay only the minimum amount and are stuck paying this debt indefinitely.

Large student loans are a killer of all opportunity. They prevent someone from starting a business, investing for retirement, and taking the necessary risks to advance their career. Imagine the pressure one would face having to quickly get a job and start paying on their $400 a month loan. They would be pressured to take the first job available even if they would be best served to wait for a better job. Also, they might be afraid to ask for that raise or be more demanding in fear that they would get fired and not be able to pay their debt. They might not look for a better job with more opportunities for growth because of fearing the higher responsibilities could lead to unemployment resulting in their debt not getting paid. They definitely wouldn't have any disposable income to put towards retirement, investments, or vacations since everything extra was going towards their loan. If someone wants to start a business, they might as well give up on that dream until their loan is paid off. The risk is too high that if the business didn't work out, they would be left with an even larger loan balance.

Do you dream of getting married, starting a family, and buying a home? Many millennials with a large student debt delay getting married and starting a family either because they want to wait until they are financially secure or because their significant other doesn't want to marry into debt. Other than having a hard time saving up for a down payment, buying a house could be problematic because the debt-income ratio might be too high to qualify for a bank loan.

The risk that comes along with having student loans is real. While many people think there is a risk in not going to college, they don't realize just how risky going to college and taking on debt is too. Too much college can quickly lead to too much debt, and ruin lives forever. This can easily be one of the riskiest investments a person could make.

The Not so Good Learning Environment

Do you think college professors provide the best education possible? I would hope so, but sometimes they put other priorities first. College professors don't get promoted on how well they teach or how much their students know but get promoted and earn more by doing research for the university. This, in turn, helps the university receive more government funding and gain prestige. This system incentivizes professors to prioritize research over teaching resulting in a poor learning environment.

The system that students are supposed to learn in is pretty simple yet not the best. Students go to class two to three times a week to hear a lecture given by an instructor to a large number of students. The lecture is normally based on a chapter in a textbook that students are expected to take notes on. Due to the large class, students who don't understand something normally won't interrupt or prolong the lecture to ask questions. The students are then expected to learn from the textbook or do assignments to help learn the material for the test. For many, the class is no better than watching a recorded video that can't even be replayed. The teacher and school have very little to do with the interactive piece that is so valuable for learning. This doesn't even take into account the rising amount of part-time adjunct professors being hired by the schools to reduce their costs. These teachers aren't paid as well and often have another job outside of teaching, so they don't care as much about the quality of education they are providing to the students. I have a friend who is studying criminal justice at a public university in Georgia. He told me how his class is online, and the teacher works full-time in the field. There was no interaction with the teacher or other students, and his only assignment was to read the textbook and submit a weekly quiz which often took weeks to be graded. He said he spent less than an hour every week on the class and after he completed the class, he confirmed that he learned close to nothing, yet still passed.

Another problem is the context of the information students learn. The majority of students are right out of high school and have no real-world experience to help them relate to what they are learning in the classroom. In other words, this new information has nearly no connection to what students already know. This is a problem since almost all learning happens through analogy, which is just the comparison of previous knowledge to new knowledge that someone is trying to acquire. Without having this real-world knowledge connection, it makes it much harder to learn the material and have an interest in it. For example, learning about economics and the supply and demand curve probably isn't of interest to most students since they don't have experience with any real-world examples to compare it to.

I remember going into an Econ 101 lecture about the supply and demand curve. Almost all the students in the class were asleep due to their lack of interest since they had no real-world knowledge to compare it to. The teacher understood very well that the students had no interest in actually learning the material, so she told the class exactly what they needed to know just to pass the test. This makes the "education" worthless for the students since they don't actually understand the concepts and will forget everything they learned.

Irrelevant and Outdated Information

One of the biggest problems with college is that, in most cases, the information students are learning is either irrelevant or outdated when it comes to getting a job in a given field. There are multiple reasons why colleges are behind the curve when it comes to teaching updated and relevant material.

The reason the information taught in college is often irrelevant is because many people choose majors that have no real-world application or jobs behind them. These types of majors should have warning labels telling people that after learning these subjects, they will likely not get a job in this field. A good name for learning these types of subjects could be "recreational learning." Some examples of this type of learning are gender studies, religious studies, or anthropology. To give some context, there are estimated to be around 400,000 anthropology degree holders, yet there are only a little over 8,000 anthropologists working in the US with only an estimated 589 positions to be added by 2026. This makes it extremely unlikely for someone majoring in the field of anthropology to actually get a job in it. If you've ever heard someone joke about majoring in underwater basket weaving, it's because they are referring to fields like this that just don't exist in the real world. As far as starting a career, it's important to remember that if you are learning about a job that doesn't exist, then you aren't doing much more than just getting a piece of paper.

The reason the information taught in college is often outdated is because many of the teachers have no real-world experience in the subject, and most of what they're teaching was from their schooling 10-50 years ago. With the world changing at a very fast pace, it has become nearly impossible for professors and textbooks to keep up. This is especially true if you want to learn a fast-changing technical profession. The fact that teachers can become tenured, allowing them to teach as long as they want without being fired, makes this problem even worse. A teacher could be teaching a subject about the internet that they have little experience with since they have been teaching since the 70s way before the internet existed.

A good example of this would be a professor teaching students about marketing and the different forms of print and radio advertising. While marketing is still a very high demand field that has many open jobs, this information might have only been relevant 20 years ago. It is now very outdated as marketing has completely changed to a more technical and analytical job. If a professor did want to teach the relevant and updated version of what marketing is today, then they would be very unqualified to do so since they never actually did it themselves or had to learn about it in depth.

Myths and False Expectations

There was a study done with more than 2,300 undergraduates that found over 45 percent of students show no significant improvement in the key measures of critical thinking, complex reasoning and writing by the end of their sophomore year. Even after four years of school, over 36 percent of students showed no significant improvement.

A myth you might have heard is that since everyone has a bachelor's degree, you need one too since it's like the new high school diploma. This is called degree inflation. College used to be very valuable since not everyone had a degree, so having one would make you stand out to companies. Now, nearly everyone has a degree, so the value of it has gone way down since having one doesn't make you stand out. A good analogy for this would be someone making a salary of $10,000 a year in the 1960s, and it is seen as a respectable wage. Now in 2019, if someone makes $10,000 a year, it is seen as poverty. This is due to inflation causing a larger amount of money to circulate in our economy and thus lowering the value of each dollar. This is the same for college degrees. In the 1960s, having any college degree put you in a rare class of people who had degrees. Now in 2019, there is an enormous number of people with college degrees circulating in our economy. This degree inflation has dramatically lowered the value of a college degree just as currency inflation lowered the value of the dollar.

This also makes the opposite true. Since there aren't many entry-level people with relevant experience or knowledge, having it makes a person stand out to companies compared to everyone else with a degree, but no relevant experience. Having just a few months of relevant experience could easily get someone more interviews than having a common college degree. I personally experienced this when I specialized my education in the sales development role with just one month of learning. This allowed me to stand out compared to all the other people who had degrees, but no knowledge of the role.

A common myth that is spread around by outdated teachers it that college is the only real post-secondary education, aka "higher education." These teachers have a hard time realizing that there are many ways to continue your education after high school with college being just one of them. Any book or blog read, or video watched are all post-secondary education. If someone were to add up all the learning that happens after high school, I would be willing to bet that college makes up less than 5%. Remember that higher education is not college. It is anything, and everything learned after high school.

Colleges sell students on the dream that after four years and majoring in something that interests them, they will get a good job and quickly pay off all their debt. This college degree is a straight shot to a nice career and the middle-class American dream. This is very different from reality. Here are the facts.

- Pew Research found that only 56% of college students graduate with a degree. This means that for the other 44%, all the money and time spent on college would be close to worthless. For those that do graduate, on average, it takes six years.

- There is an average student loan default rate of 11%. This means that 11% of people stop paying their student loans, which results in lowering their credit score and accumulating interest. The government can also take the loan payment right out of their paycheck. Some studies have predicted that as many as 40% of students could be defaulting on their loans by 2023

- A study by Strada Institute found that more than 40% of college students are currently taking jobs that don't require degrees and CareerBuilder did their own study and found this number to be over 51%. This doesn't even take into account the large percentage of jobs classified as college jobs that can still be gotten without a degree. Nor does it take into account the 31% of graduates not employed after three months.

- A study by Jaison R. Abel and Richard Deitz found that only 27% of college graduates are working in jobs that were closely related to their college major. One study found that fewer than 1 in 5000 graduates with a marketing degree got their first job that closely related to what they learned in school. What people don't know is that to get a "traditional marketing" job, you first need sales experience, which is why over 88% of marketing majors start their first job in sales. A study at Harvard found that more than 50% of US college graduates, regardless of their majors, are likely to work in sales at some point.

• In 2013 the bureau of labor statistics released a snapshot of minimum wage workers that showed there are over 260,000 people with bachelor's degrees working for a minimum wage of $7.25 an hour and an additional 200,000 people with associate degrees also working for the minimum wage.

You might also hear studies talk about how much better the lives of college graduates are compared to high school graduates. This could include things like committing less crime or having a higher average income, etc. This is a common marketing tactic used to convince students that college is valuable. The reason this is so misleading is that most people have a hard time deciphering between causation versus correlation. For example, if your grandma cooks really good pie and always uses a cast iron pot, do you think the cast iron pot is what's making the pie so good, or could it be the ingredients she uses and the way she cooks it? The cast-iron pot just happens to be correlated with everything else. Another example of causation versus correlation is Whole Foods. On average, the people that shop at Whole Foods make over $100,000 a year. This means that shopping at Whole Foods is one of the best things you can do if you want to make six figures and break into the upper-middle class, right? It's important to question whether shopping at Whole Foods cause people to make more money or if there is a correlation between high-income people that shop at Whole Foods. If these same people decided to stop shopping at Whole Foods, then would their incomes drop?

The same is true of college. For the most part, college isn't the cause of what makes someone commit less crime or make more money. It's the correlation with the type of people who go to college versus the type of people who don't. The type of people going to college as a whole are more motivated and more educated than those not going to college because society has made them think college is the best way to get ahead in life. This is why these statistics are very skewed. If you took two people who had the same motivation and the same level of education when graduating high school, yet one went to college and one didn't, the statistics would be much different. Perhaps we might even have more innovation from people who had the freedom to pursue their dreams instead of a 4-year degree.

One statistic that is thrown around a lot is that college graduates make over 1 million dollars more over a lifetime. I bet Whole Foods shoppers also make 1 million more over a lifetime compared to shoppers at Walmart. Does that mean if these Walmart shoppers start shopping at Whole Foods, then they too will make 1 million more over a lifetime? I don't think so. This statistic doesn't even take into account the money spent or the debt accumulated going to college. Just from a pure investment perspective, the money saved by not going to college could simply be put into an S&P 500 index fund. By retirement, it would be worth over $12 million, which is a much better return on investment than college.

Inefficient and Ineffective 4 Year Model

The entire 4-year model that colleges use actually breeds a huge number of inefficiencies while also being a very ineffective way to start a career. Who came up with the idea that it takes everyone 4 years to become competent? Why do people think a traditional education is so important? Is technology traditional? Are our jobs traditional? Is our economy traditional? Has nothing changed in the last 100 years that might require a different way of learning?

I like to start this section off by reminding everyone that the focus of this book is on education that leads to jobs and successful careers. There are lots of interesting things people can learn that don't necessarily lead to getting a job. My goal is not to convince people to stop learning about subjects that don't lead to jobs, but instead be able to classify the education as recreational learning versus career learning. My definition of recreational learning is learning for the sake of interest or for your personal development. Career learning, on the other hand, is learning for the sake of starting or advancing your career. The traditional 4-year college model has really confused the general population on the difference between the two.

First Two Years of General Study

Let's start with the first two years of a college education. These first two years, classified as general education, include English, math, science, history, etc. Most of these subjects were already taught in high school with much overlap. Why do students need to learn about basic biology all over again if they already learned about it in high school? Did the biology of a microorganism change, or is it really that important for non-biology majors to know? What about the Latin history class? Did the world history class in high school not go in-depth enough, and students need to spend all their money and time to learn about Latin history in college? There are three main reasons general education classes are a waste.

The first reason is that while many people might argue that these things are good to know, the fact is that learning biology 101 isn't going to get someone a job in business or even biology. The same can be said for nearly every class someone takes during their first two years of general education. How many people do you know that have said their Biology 101 or Econ 101 class really contributed to their career success and still remember all the material? Out of all the people I've asked this question, I've never found anyone who still remembered everything unless the class was part of their major. Another thing to note is that anything someone can google and learn in a matter of minutes, such as facts or formulas, is useless to try to remember. No one will ever hire someone for this type of knowledge. Being able to do effective research and find answers on any topic you need at a given time is much more important than trying to remember things in hopes it might be useful at a later date. If someone actually needed to know something from biology 101 five years down the line, they probably would have forgotten pretty much everything and would need to cherry-pick the information from a few google searches.

Imagine a boss asking one of their employees to solve a math problem. One employee tries to do it on paper and another employee copies and pastes it into google. The person who put it into google got the answer 10x faster than the person who did it by hand. In real life, it's just about getting the results. The person who can get the most accurate results the fastest is the person who will get the promotion.

General education has become more useless because our economy has become much more specialized, making jobs also much more specialized. This has made being a jack of all trades or a generalist extremely hard since jobs today require a much more in-depth, complex, and specialized skill set. Adam

Smith very accurately talked about this in his book, *The Wealth of Nations*, which was published in 1776. He went in-depth about a concept, called the division of labor, where the separation of a work process into a number of tasks, with each task performed by a separate person or group of persons, will improve efficiency. A good example of this would be the software programming field. Thirty years ago, someone may have started a career as just a programmer, but now there are many specialized programming jobs. There are front end developers, back end developers, security, etc. Just being a general programmer is probably too broad to even get a job now.

The second reason general education classes are a waste is because they are not a good foundation to build upon, although many people will argue that they are. Building an education on a solid foundation is very important. I'd even go so far to say that it is just as important as building a house on a solid foundation. For most people, trying to build on top of general education courses is like building a house on sand. The sand will crumble, and your general education will too.

General education isn't a good foundation because knowledge spoils just like milk spoils when left out. If you've ever heard people say knowledge is power, then they didn't tell you the whole phrase. Knowledge is only powerful if it is used. Knowledge is also only retained if it is used. Can you think about things you learned in school a couple of years ago or perhaps even just a couple months ago, but already have forgotten nearly everything about? I can almost guarantee the reason you forgot it is because you didn't use it. This means that most of the general education that people learn will spoil and perish away since it is not used. What kind of foundation is that?

Most people learn new things through analogy. This basically means that people use previously known knowledge to interpret and rationalize new information they want to learn. An example of this could be someone who wants to learn about what an antagonist is. Instead of just learning what it is by reading the definition of how it is someone who opposes another person, it would be much easier to learn what it is through an analogy with previously known knowledge.

An example of an analogy could be using a sport someone is familiar with, such as lifting weights, to teach why consistency in work is important. This could be talking about how someone who goes to the gym and has a hard workout for two days, then takes a week off will not make nearly as many gains as someone who has a moderate workout, but for weeks straight. This person knows that consistency is the most important factor for gym success, so they can use it to relate to why consistency is also the most important factor for success at work. This example I just gave about learning through analogies is actually an analogy itself. I would go so far to say that all learning happens through analogy with much of it being subconscious. Any time someone is trying to learn something new, their mind is constantly finding ways to connect it to previously known information to understand and rationalize it. The theory for this way of learning is called constructivism. Wikipedia's definition is "Constructivism in education is an epistemological perspective of learning focused on how students actively create (or "construct") knowledge out of their experiences. Emphasis is placed on agency and prior "knowing" and experience of the learner, which is often determined by their social and cultural contexts environment."

The reason this relates to using general education to build a foundation is because most college freshmen or sophomores don't have any real-world experience to use as analogies to learn many of these general subjects. This leads to people not having a strong understanding of the underlying concepts, but instead only learning bits of information that is required for their tests. This makes it so their knowledge of the subjects is forgotten even faster without use and they can't use their knowledge of these general subjects as analogies for learning other more complex material since they don't have a deep understanding of it. This is because learning through analogies only works if the person already has a strong understanding of the knowledge they are using to interpret new information. These analogies are built on top of one another and having weak ones at the bottom is what creates that poor foundation. It is instead much more beneficial to have a more focused, yet stronger understanding of the knowledge you are using as analogies to relate new information to. This is what creates a strong foundation to build on. Someone with more real-life experience who learns about some of these general subjects will be able to relate their experiences to it, which allows for much easier and deeper understanding. This can be clearly seen in subjects like history and economics where most adults have experienced it firsthand, allowing them to learn much faster.

The last reason that general education classes are a waste is because they are not good for helping students figure out what to do as a career, although many people might try to argue they are. Students probably already dabbled in most of these subjects during high school. If they didn't find they had any interest in it back in high school, then they probably won't have any interest in it now. An example of this could be math. If a student was never good at math and hated it in high school, then they will probably still not want to major in it during college. The opposite is also true. If they really enjoyed math during high school, yet hated English, they will probably still enjoy doing something involving math instead of English in their career.

Another problem with using these general education studies to try to figure out what to major in and do for your career is that these studies often don't relate to any real-world entry-level jobs. This means that even if you take an economics class and enjoy the material, you probably won't actually be able to relate that material to any real entry-level job that you could get out of college. I know a girl who took multiple English classes and enjoys writing. She planned on majoring in English until she learned that the actual types of jobs she would be able to do after she graduated are much different than the type of writing she enjoys. These misconceptions are a big part of what contributes to the expectations versus reality gap that students go through after they graduate college.

Universities actually have a very invested interest in making sure people take these introductory classes. These classes are often by far the biggest profit center for the universities. With their very large class size in the lecture halls and perhaps just one or two paid staff in the room, they make a lot of money from these classes. This profit is actually what pays for their unprofitable classes that have a much lower student to staff ratio or require expensive equipment. Many universities are now offering online education for these introductory classes, which further increase class size and lower expenses, yet they are still charging the same amount of money.

Last Two Years of Major Study

The second part to the traditional four-year college model is the last two years. These last two years of college are normally composed of major-specific classes that will lead to a specific degree. For example, these could be mechanical engineering classes that will get someone a mechanical engineering degree, or they could be an array of finance and marketing classes that lead to a business degree. One major problem with taking these classes is that students are required to spend two years of their time and money doing recreational learning before they can even get to the point of being able to take these classes. This is the case even if the major a student picks has little or nothing to do with the general education courses. I will classify the problems with these last two years of study into two categories — the inefficiency and ineffectiveness.

The inefficiency can be described as all the things that cause wasted time, money, and resources. The first reason that makes these classes so inefficient is that students don't know what they want to major in and often pick something at near-random. If students commit two years learning about a subject and end up not getting a job in that field, then most of that education is wasted, causing huge inefficiencies. Many people like psychology and choose to major in it, but do not become psychologists. Likewise, many students who major in marketing do not become marketers. Most students, even after two years of general education classes, aren't really sure about what they want to do. This, coupled with the pressure from universities to choose a major, leads to students making poor decisions on what they are committing the next two years of their time and money to.

It should be morally unacceptable to pressure young 18-20-year-olds into making such a large life decision at such a high cost of time and money. I know countless people who choose a random major just to continue in college and get that college degree. I met a guy who thought he would like engineering, so he went to a great engineering school and studied hard to graduate with a high GPA to only realize that he didn't want to become an engineer. He now enjoys painting houses, but the debt taken on from his college years makes it very hard for him to be able to focus on doing work he enjoys instead of focusing on the pay. This same scenario replays over and over as people realize that they don't like the work they studied for in college, but feel trapped since they need to keep working in their job to pay off their debt which could easily last until they are in their 30s.

Another reason that causes huge inefficiencies is that the job people actually get after graduation might only use a fraction of what they learned. This could be as little as 1-5%, making someone's education 95-99% inefficient. This is because the material students learn in college often has very little overlap with real-world application or is outdated. As an example, if someone really enjoys marketing and wants to work in that field after they graduate with a marketing degree, the actual real-world job is often much different than what they thought it would be like from class. Some people decide not to continue working in their career field after learning how different the real world is from their perception causing over 99% inefficiency. Other people who continue to pursue a job in their career field have been taught outdated information that isn't used on the job causing over 95% inefficiency. Could you imagine how long a manufacturing company would be able to stay in business if their process was over 95% inefficient? With the world changing at such a fast pace, it makes it extremely hard for teachers to even come close to staying relevant to reduce this inefficiency.

The Ineffectiveness can be described as a college's inability to get a student a good job in their field of study. The first reason college is very ineffective at getting students a good job in the major they studied for the last two years is due to competition. With the majority of recent high school graduates going to college now, there has become a huge influx in the number of applicants applying to basically the same number of jobs. This has caused a very high level of competition for these "college-level" jobs, especially now, since nearly everyone applies online with just a click of a button. This makes the recruiters at these companies have to scan through vast amounts of resumes. Unless a student went to a top school, their college degree is going to do little in differentiating them from the other college graduates.

Another reason for a college's ineffectiveness is that for many fields of study, the number of available jobs is significantly less than the number of people studying it. A good example of this would be sociology. The Bureau of Labor Statistics says the number of sociology jobs is 3,500 with an expected job growth of 0-1% in the next ten years. Out of these 3,500 jobs, most, if not all of them, are already filled with qualified people. The number of people graduating with sociology degrees is nearly 37,000 every year. This means that out of the 37,000 graduates, there will likely only be less than ten every year that actually get a job in sociology. The other 36,990 graduates won't be getting a job in sociology and will be competing for other jobs that don't even utilize what they learned. Other than this being very inefficient, it is also ineffective. Companies realize they have to train recent graduates from the ground up regardless of their major, so companies put very little to no value on which degree students have for most entry-level white-collar jobs. This makes nearly all applications from recent graduates for these jobs look identical to recruiters. There was actually a study done for entry-level sales roles which further proved this by showing that there was no significant difference in performance based on their college major other than engineering majors who performed slightly better in the aggregate.

Imagine a recruiter that is in charge of recruiting for an entry-level assistant position that pays $35,000 a year. Within the first day of posting the position, there are already over 100 applicants, and by the end of the week, there are nearly 500. There is no way they can interview all these applicants, so they look for signals that would help them identify which people are the most qualified for the position. They know the position requires people to do many different tasks, but there isn't a major that trains people how to be assistants. The closest skills that affect the success of their work would be great interpersonal skills, writing skills, and being very detail oriented. They also have to use signals to help identify which people actually want this position and are not applying just to get a job. Their level of interest and desire will dictate how hard they will work to be the best and how long they will stay at the company. Both of which are incredibly important. This means the two biggest factors recruiters are looking for in recent graduates are their qualifications to do the job effectively and interest in making a career out of the role.

A great signal to identify which applicants are probably the most qualified for this role are people who have college degrees. Out of the 500 applicants, they assume the people with degrees probably have better interpersonal, writing, and detail-oriented skills than people without degrees. The second thing they look for are people who went to top universities since they probably have better skills than people who went to lower-tier universities. If they saw anyone who went to a top university, they would probably schedule an interview with them since they are likely very qualified, and it would be worth their time to figure out their level of interest in the position. Even after filtering out everyone who doesn't have a degree, they probably still have at least 250 applicants left. They then spend under 20 seconds scanning each resume to help find different signals such as work experience, accomplishments, and relevant education, which would prove someone has these qualifications and interest to be an assistant. This means that the effectiveness of a college degree alone to get a general entry-level job only gets you to second base where you still must separate yourself from the other 250 applicants.

Free College?

There is an idea going around at the time of this writing that free college for everyone is a good idea. It is actually a terrible idea in the current state of our college system. This is due to the inefficiency that would skyrocket if it was free. Imagine how many more people would go to college just for the heck of it if it didn't cost anything. These people wouldn't care about making the most of their time or putting in the effort to start a career afterward. They would just be going to get that college experience while they figure out what they actually want to do. I would bet that this would drive the average inefficiency of using college to start a career up over 99%.

Free college would also affect the people that didn't plan on going to college in the first place. The people who were planning to go into the trades or were going to do something else wouldn't do it anymore. Why should they? If it's the free, fun, and cool thing that all their friends are doing, then why not? If they didn't go, then they would still have to pay for everyone else to go to college in the form of taxes. That wouldn't seem fair. Without people going into fields that don't require college, it would drive the price of services such as construction, plumbing, and manufacturing way up. Perhaps even to a price that would make it hard for the middle and lower class to afford. Free college would also make college degrees even more worthless because anyone and everyone would have one. It would come to the point that just a week's worth of specialized education would be more valuable than a college degree for many jobs. Fast food restaurants' new qualification might require a college degree or one month's worth of work experience.

Other than how poorly a college degree would result in getting a good job, imagine how much more inefficient colleges would use the money they get. If colleges get funding based on the number of students enrolled, then they would just ramp up their spending on what attracts students. This means that for all the students who are just going for the experience, then colleges would just further spend on the experience and less on the education. This combined with lowered academic standards to accommodate every level would lower the overall quality of the education for the few students who actually want to learn.

The only reason the free college system works at all in some other countries such as Germany and Sweden is because their system is much different than ours. In Germany they actually separate kids based on their abilities and desired path at the end of 4th grade. This is what keeps the number of people studying different careers in line with their economic demands by limiting how many people can even go to college. Their college experience isn't all that different from the apprenticeship experience either. They don't have a party culture, sports teams, or fraternities and sororities. The government doesn't pay for much of anything experience-wise as the only thing they provide is the education. This is why so many people opt to choose apprenticeships over college as there isn't a big difference in the fun or cool factor.

The idea of free college in the US actually stems from the belief that education is a right and is desirable for our society to have educated people. I firmly believe everyone should have the opportunity to educate themselves. With our modern world giving free or affordable access to education for anyone who wants to learn, it's no longer necessary for the government to be involved in funding colleges to achieve this goal. Education already is accessible to anyone who wants to learn.

3

The Modern Education Generation

There have been fundamental shifts in the way the new generation of young people go about learning. Not too long ago, people didn't have nearly the same amount of resources to learn from as they do today. My parents often said how lucky I was to be able to learn the way I did, yet I never realized just how fortunate I was until I researched what learning used to entail. Nearly everything we know about education and work has been affected by the advent of the internet.

Growing Up with Online Education

Millennials, born between 1981 and 1996, started high school between 1995 and 2010. In 1995 the internet was just taking off with companies like AltaVista as the search engine. For these people, the internet wasn't much help for learning their high school material as the internet was still in its infancy. For the Millennials who entered high school in 2010, they were on the cusp of the growth of learning content on the internet. In 2010, websites, like YouTube, started experiencing exponential growth of their content base along with other companies like

Khan Academy who got funding as a non-profit to develop a full k-12 curriculum that could teach the world for free. The number of blogs and other learning resources started exploding in 2010. Some of the Millennials who were beginning high school at this time adapted to this new technology and were able to use online learning content to assist with their schooling.

Things start to get really interesting when we look at Generation Z. This generation, born between 1997 and 2012, started high school in 2011. By 2011 there was a huge growth in the number of teens who had access to the internet through their smartphones alongside exponential growth in the amount of online learning content. This was when online learning became a mainstream way to help assist or even be a full alternative for the freshmen entering high school. These freshmen were able to learn anything they wanted about any of their classes. If they had a question about how to do a particular math problem, instead of asking the teacher to explain it again, they could simply google it and watch an online tutorial on how to solve it. It even became possible to miss weeks or months of class at a time and just have the class outline to learn the material on their own.

An excellent example of this is when I entered high school in 2012. I found it much easier to learn online as the lectures were more thought out and in-depth than anything my high school teachers could plan. It was also effortless to replay a lecture if needed or instantly dig deeper into a particular subject with a simple Google search. In a fraction of the time, I learned the material better than even some of the smartest people in my class. This enabled me to confidently bypass class and still maintain a very satisfactory GPA. There are actually many schools now offering online schooling as a mainstream option. I've noticed many of my younger peers are now doing most of their schooling online as they also realized they learned better online. A study between years 2013 - 2014 found there to be well over 300,000 full-time online k-12 students and over 2.7 million blended online learning k-12 students.

The part of Generation Z, which was born after the year 2000, only remember learning with the assistance of the internet. It is fundamentally ingrained in the way they learn. This new way of learning is also starting to enter the workforce. The oldest people of Generation Z, now 22 years old, will start showing other people in the workforce the powerful skill of being able to learn anything they want at a very fast pace online. Very soon, these same people will also be the managers at many of these companies in charge of hiring other people from Generation Z and beyond. These managers understand that most learning happens outside of the classroom and will use skills and ability as the new way to go about assessing talent instead of formal education.

The Global Sharing Economy

Another significant impact that the internet has had is the ease at which people can share information. Not too long ago if someone wanted to share their opinion, they would have to get on the news. Now people can write a blog on a website like Medium or send a tweet out to the world with the click of a button. If someone wants to write a book, they don't need to find a publisher to be able to produce and market it as they can now self-publish their own book for free and market it themselves through social media. If an expert on a particular subject wants to publish their teachings to the world, they can easily do so on YouTube or an array of online course websites. There are also websites like Quora which allow people to easily share questions and get answers from some of the smartest people in the world. The internet has also allowed people to do more than just share information. Companies like Uber and Airbnb are good examples of mainstream companies that utilize the internet to enable people to share their transportation or housing.

The way the sharing economy has dramatically impacted learning is through the use of scale. Most subjects, such as math and history, are identical from class to class. This means that one teacher could invest much more time in teaching the most effective and best-planned lecture as it can be recorded as a video and shared all over the world to teach millions of people for many years to come. The only other point in history that had as big of an impact as this does for teaching is the advent of the book. Someone could write a book which could be copied and shipped all over the world to teach millions of people. This allowed people to learn from others irrespective of their location. An expert on a particular subject could write a book in one country, and someone in another country could read it and learn from them. Before the book, the only way to learn was from someone in person. This made new information much harder to pick up and implement around the world due to how slowly it spread. When technology such as the printing press allowed books to be mass-produced, it lowered the cost of books and also greatly impacted the speed at which information spread.

The internet is having the same effect on the ability for new information to spread. Until the internet took off, learning information outside of class was mostly from books in paper form. With the internet, we also have video lectures, live discussions, question answering, instant research ability, and up to date eBooks. Now with the internet, new ideas are continuously being spread all over the world every second. If someone had to choose between in class without the internet or the internet without class, the internet would almost always come out on top, giving the best possible education.

A good example of this for K-12 education would be Khan Academy. Sal Khan has produced an entire set of perfected teaching material that is open for everyone in the world to learn from. This means that someone in the poorest parts of India can be getting the same level of education from someone in the wealthiest parts of America. Khan Academy has over 100 million people learning from their teachings every year. To give some reference to the scale of this number, Sal Khan is teaching more students than every teacher in the United States combined.

Another example of online education is MOOCs. These stand for Massive Open Online Courses. There are companies such as Coursera or Udacity which publish full college courses that are either free or very low cost. These courses are taught by some of the best professors and business leaders in the world. There are universities such as Pen State's Wharton Business School that teach entire online business courses that are affordable for anyone to learn from. Think about it. Would you rather learn accounting that is taught by the smartest and most reputable business organization in the world and perfected over many years, or learn it from a teacher at your local state school? In Jeff Selingo's book *College Unbound*, he talks about how Carnegie Mellon University is in the process of developing online courses. The professors creating the courses often spend hours trying to figure out the best way to explain a single concept, something that in-class professors would never invest so much time in. Carnegie Mellon actually ran a study which compared students who took a class in person versus in an online hybrid environment. They found that students who took the online version of the class learned the same material, but in only 75 percent of the time that the other students took in the in-person class.

The last example of this that I would like to add is the ability for individual professionals to teach their expertise. There are countless people that teach their expertise in every discipline imaginable such as athletes that teach fitness and beauty professionals that teach cosmetology. There are also websites like Udemy which allow people to make money from their teachings by charging people a minimal amount for their courses. They range from online marketing experts teaching search engine optimization courses to business analyst experts teaching courses on using Excel.

In all these cases, the ability for anyone to easily reach a large number of people with their teaching is what allows the cost to be dramatically reduced. If a teacher wants to make $50,000 a year, they only need 2,500 students paying $20 a pop to take the course. If the teacher has a hundred thousand students, the cost of the course could be reduced to 50 cents. The internet has also allowed people to learn from almost anywhere without the requirement of a physical location. This has eliminated one of the most considerable costs of modern education, which is infrastructure. Other associated costs such as textbooks can be entirely online as a living document that is continuously updated, just like apps. This eliminates printing costs for the original document and updated versions. It also makes it very easy for everyone to use the same textbook due to ease of distribution, which in turn lowers its cost by being spread out over many more students. This means the internet has significantly reduced the most significant costs associated with education: teaching, infrastructure, and books. It is safe to say that we are on track to reducing the cost of nearly all education to being easily affordable for everyone, democratizing education.

Education for Modern Careers

To be successful in the modern world, it is more important than ever to be educated. It's the type of education and the medium in which you become educated that has changed. No longer does someone have to spend tens of thousands of dollars and many years to get a world-class education. Also, no longer can someone get a general college education and expect to land a good job with it afterward. The world has changed, and people have to change along with it.

I often see people associating higher education with only college. With so much learning happening outside the classroom, the view of higher education needs to change. A better definition of higher education that I propose would be something along the lines of "continuing one's education after high school." The medium in which someone gets the education has no reason to belong in the definition. There are many ways to go about learning and becoming educated in this modern world with college being only one of many ways just like YouTube is only one of many ways. Governments need to stop using college as their statistic for describing how educated a populous is when it's such a small fraction of someone's education nowadays.

The other part of education that has changed is the type of education that is valuable in today's economy. With the world becoming much more complex, so have jobs. As I mentioned earlier about the division of labor, as the world becomes more complex, then all jobs will become more specialized to improve efficiency. To be able to produce a minimum amount of value in a job, a person needs to have a very particular skill set. Not too long ago, someone could graduate with a very general degree and expect a company to train them after they are hired, but not anymore. Today's companies prefer employees that can already produce value in their role from day one. They are not looking to place someone in a position and invest heavily in them with the hopes they will enjoy it, be successful, and stay at the company for many years to come. This has become a particular problem since most college graduates learn something far too general to actually produce even a minimum amount of value in a good paying entry-level job.

Many of the high paying jobs in our economy today are skill-based often involving the use of technology. Instead of needing someone to do all the work a piece of technology can do, we now need people who know how to use that technology to get their desired outcome. A great example of how middle-class jobs have changed over the years is in an industry like manufacturing where it has changed from skilled tradespeople building multiple components to technicians managing the robots and automation that each performs a very simple task. Many of these jobs are not taught in school because our economy is changing way too fast and creating too many new types of jobs for schools to keep up with. Just a few of these new jobs in a career like marketing that didn't exist just a little over ten years ago would be jobs like social media manager, SEO specialist, content creator, etc. The list goes on and on.

Lifelong Learning

There has been another significant change in the way people structure their learning. In the past, people were under the mindset that if they went to college for four years, they would be able to work in their career field until retirement without any additional education. This kind of mindset was much more feasible back then as the pace at which the world changed was much slower, allowing people not to have to continuously learn to stay relevant. That has all changed. Now, continuous lifelong learning isn't only encouraged; it's required. No longer can someone expect to learn everything at once and be done learning. There will be new changes and inventions that affect their work, requiring to learn new information.

Let's take the medical field for example. If someone wants to become a doctor, they have to commit to lifelong learning. Imagine a doctor spending 12 years in school learning about medicine before opening his practice, yet he doesn't learn anything for the next 20 years. During these 20 years, many new diseases and medicine to heal these diseases have been uncovered, yet this doctor doesn't know anything about them. Would you want to be the patient that he falsely diagnoses or can't prescribe the proper medication because he didn't continue his education?

Every industry is changing faster than ever. As technology evolves and new techniques are developed for different processes, the way people do their jobs and the education required to do that job continuously changes. In this modern world, people have to commit to lifelong learning if they want to have a successful long-term career.

Why Some Careers Pay Better Than Others

Have you ever wondered why some jobs pay much less than others even when the lesser paying job is harder? There are two main factors which impact how much money a position will pay. The first is the market value of what you're doing, and the second is the supply and demand for it.

The market value for a role is based on the amount of impact the role has. In business, this means if the role has the ability to make or save a company ten million dollars, then the market value for that role is ten times greater than a different role which only has the ability to affect one million dollars. For a role such as artificial intelligence programming, there are people getting paid in the high six figures due to the significant impact they can have on a company's valuation. Another type of job that has high market value is oil rig work. The average salary across all oil rig workers is about $100,000 a year. This is heavily due to the large market impact these workers have. This is because one oil rig could easily produce 100,000 barrels of oil a day and over 36 million barrels a year. With oil being worth over $60 a barrel this would put the amount of revenue at over $2 billion a year for one rig. With less than 100 people working on a rig, this makes each person's job imperative that they do it right since it has such a huge impact.

For other roles, the impact is often tied to how much leverage someone has. For people that work in finance, this leverage is usually based on the amount of other people's money they have under their control. This could mean that a hedge fund manager who gives a fund a 15% return a year on 100 million dollars doesn't have nearly the impact as another hedge fund manager who gives a 15% return on 100 billion dollars. The person who has 1000 times the amount of financial leverage could presumably get paid 1000 times more. The more common type of leverage that is present in nearly all businesses is management. This is the leverage of other people's time and ability. If you have ever wondered why CEOs or executives make so much money, it's because the impact they have is amplified by the number of people they have working for them. This means that the impact of a single decision a CEO makes could be amplified by their 10,000 employees to either make the company significant amounts of money or lose significant amounts. This is why it's not strange to find CEOs of large corporations making in excess of $100 million a year.

The other part of the equation that affects how much a role pays is the supply and demand for it. This is one of the most basic factors in economics, which means that as demand goes up, then prices go up if supply is the same (Demand > Supply). It could also be reversed where if supply goes down, then prices will go up if demand stays the same (Supply < Demand).

An excellent example of a role where demand has significantly outpaced supply would be in computer programming. There has been a massive influx in demand as large amounts of money have been poured into internet companies. This has created more jobs than there are qualified workers making companies compete to attract talent by increasing wages. This increase in demand also affects the speed at which people get promoted. This is due to the fact that more demand usually means more entry-level hiring leading to existing employees getting promoted faster.

A different example of where it's actually the supply which has gone down would be the trades. This is often why you will see people talking about how we need more tradespeople and the high pay often associated with them. I believe the main driver for the decrease in supply is due to most young people being pushed into a traditional 4-year university instead of a trade school or apprenticeship. This has made it so that even if demand is stagnant, the wages for these trade roles are still increasing due to the low amount of supply. Mike Rowe, the star on Dirty Jobs, has found that unattractive jobs often pay exceptionally well since the supply of people willing to do it is so low. He is trying very hard to make people aware of these high paying career options that lie in the trades due to this shortage of qualified talent. A decrease in supply can also be caused by government regulation, which makes it harder for people in law, insurance, medicine, etc. to get licensed to work in a field, therefore, increasing wages.

A perfect example where demand has gone up simultaneously with supply going down would be truck driving. The demand has rapidly gone up due to the increase in e-commerce shipping. The supply has gone down due to the unattractiveness of the job, along with most of the younger generation being pushed to college. This is what has allowed truck drivers to make in excess of $100,000 a year in a relatively low skill job.

4

The Lean Career Model

How do we use these new changes in the world to solve the problems with our current education system? The answer is to create a new model for our modern world. The new model must account for the new types of jobs available in today's economy and the required education to do these jobs effectively. It must also consider the rapid pace of change that is affecting nearly everything we do and must utilize modern ways of learning to provide the best education at the least cost. This new model is called The Lean Career.

What Is Lean

Lean is most commonly described as something being minimal or without waste. In the meat department, people would generally use lean to describe meat without fat or in bodybuilding lean would describe people without fat. In business, lean is often referred to as the efficiency of one's operation, such as manufacturing. The term, lean manufacturing, was created by the engineers at Toyota and defined as "A systematic method for the minimization of waste within a manufacturing system without sacrificing productivity, which can cause problems. Lean also factors in waste created through overburden and waste created through unevenness in workloads. Working from the perspective of the client who consumes a product or service, "value" is any action or process that a customer would be willing to pay for. Lean manufacturing attempts to make obvious what adds value, through reducing everything else (because it is not adding value)."

There are many different types of lean models people follow for everything from starting companies and software development to manufacturing and distribution. Each industry that implemented lean was able to figure out its core fundamental value so it could focus all its efforts on improving that value while reducing everything else that doesn't add value. In software development, people realized that the fundamental value comes from creating software that people want. When creating software, even if you are able to deliver it on time and without bugs, it is completely wasted if no one wants it. This realization caused people to change their mindset to prioritize and make sure they are developing something people want instead of it just being high quality or on time. This allowed for a new model in software development known as agile development.

One of the only industries I found that doesn't use any type of lean model is the education industry. My guess as to why is that there has always been a seemingly endless amount of money coming from the government in the form of student loans and subsidies, so universities never needed to worry about efficiency or reducing waste. They also never needed to worry about the value to their students, since they got paid no matter how much or how little the student actually learned or if the student could find a job or not after graduating. The goals of universities are not aligned with the majority of students, whose primary goals are to start a good-paying career without having to go into debt.

My definition for The Lean Career is: "A scientific model for starting or advancing a career, with that being the core value. This model focuses on the minimization of educational waste and uses modern ways of learning to reduce costs. Educational waste can be described as any education that doesn't lead to starting or advancing a career. The model allows for rapidly testing careers a person hypothesizes are a good fit until they find one that they want to expand on."

The Fundamentals

The lean career was built on five fundamental concepts:

- Career as the goal
- Specializing first
- Modern learning
- Rapid testing
- Just in time education

These concepts were derived from the changes that have happened in our economy with the goal of reducing waste while improving the effectiveness of starting a successful career. These changes include the type of jobs available, the requirements to do these jobs, and the way people go about learning.

1. Career as The Goal. The first fundamental concept of the lean career is that starting a great career is the primary goal. A great career can be defined as a career that aligns with the life a person is looking to build, whether that is based on work/life balance, money, or the type of work they enjoy doing. By starting with a great career as the primary goal, it allows someone to eliminate much of the waste that occurs if one starts with the education as the goal. Most people start with the education and then search for a role where it can be used instead of starting with a career and working backward to get the required education for that career. Starting with the education is not the best way because what is taught in college is normally much different than what the job will require. This is the cause of the 90%+ inefficiency. Working backward from the goal shortens the gap between the differences in the education and the real job one gets. By learning what is directly relevant to the job, educational waste is greatly reduced. For many people that start with the education, they find that after they graduate college, there are actually no available jobs in their field of study. This risk can be entirely eliminated by starting with a career role as the goal because someone would already know what the job market for that career looks like.

I interviewed a guy named Jack, who graduated with a degree in Media Management; however, his first job out of college was in information technology sales. He said that out of the 40+ classes he took in college, there were only three classes that he recalled were even somewhat useful. This means if all three of those classes were taught perfectly, and he used 100% of what he learned in the classes, then at best, his education was about 93% inefficient. Most likely, his classes were not taught 100% efficiently, and he didn't use everything he learned in the classes. A more realistic estimate of his education's inefficiency would be 95-99%.

A good example of this in another industry would be if someone wanted to build a house and instead of working backward from a blueprint, they went out and purchased a variety of materials with the hopes of finding a way to put it all together to create a house. I'm sure this kind of construction would cause the price of the house to be many times what it would typically cost when working from a blueprint due to all the wasted materials, time, and reconstruction. It's crazy to think that people are doing this with education. This same thinking of working backward from a goal can also be used to improve nearly all aspects of someone's life. People should spend time figuring out what goals they want to pursue and then work backward to figure out what they need to do in order to accomplish that goal. If someone is not intentional about working backwards from a goal, then they are just a drifter going through the motions with no end in sight.

The idea of students starting with education first stems all the way back to students being conditioned to think that college is their goal after high school. This is a toxic mentality, since over 80% of college freshmen are in college to start a career, not just to get an education. This means that for over 80% of students out there, their goal should be to first start with the actual career they want to be doing and then work backward to get the required education to do that career.

2. Specializing First. The second fundamental concept of the lean career is to start with a very specialized education. The reason this is better is because entry-level jobs are now much more specialized due to our complex economy. Specializing goes hand and hand with having a career as the goal. This is because someone who works backward to figure out what they need to learn to break into a career will ultimately specialize their education in that one role. By specializing first, it allows someone to eliminate the educational waste that would be prevalent if they obtained a very general education, only to go into a very specialized role and end up not using everything they learned. Specialized education also helps applicants stand out to companies since all their education is directly relevant to the job, unlike their generalized peers. This makes them especially rare in many entry-level jobs where almost everyone applying is just searching for a role where they can apply their education.

Have you ever heard people say they are going to get a general degree because they can do anything with it? Unfortunately, people who do graduate with a general college degree quickly find out that anything is not much better than nothing. People can do anything with a high school diploma. They can go to college, go into the trades, travel, learn, or go straight to work. While they can do seemingly anything, they are capable of nothing. People who get a general college degree thinking they can get any job, quickly find this out when they aren't qualified to do anything.

When I was working as an account executive part of my job was to recruit another entry-level salesperson to do business to business sales. I posted job ads on nearly every job board and had hundreds of applications within just a few days. The hard qualifications for the position were minimal and out of all the applicants that applied about half of them had college degrees, making their degree a very poor differentiator. Out of the hundreds of applicants, there were only a few who had anything on their application that was even slightly relevant to the position, with the most common being some form of call center experience. No one had any education relevant to the sales role nor even internship experience in a similar role. With these two factors topping the list as the most important entry-level job indicators, it makes people who have them extremely rare and really stand out to hiring managers. I also phone screened over 15 entry-level candidates who seemed to have little to no knowledge of the role. They applied just because they graduated college with a very general degree and were looking for a job where they could use their degree. This was the case across the board. If anyone of these people had a strong understanding of the role or at least some relevant education or experience, it would have made them easily stand out.

3. Modern Learning. The third fundamental concept of the lean career is utilizing modern learning techniques. This includes advances in education such as learning online through video lectures, research, discussion forums, etc. With the new generation of students growing up with this new way of learning, it has become the preference of many. By using modern learning techniques, everyone has access to the highest quality education. Students can learn from the smartest individuals and professors in the world, which used to only be accessible to a very select number of students. This high-quality education comes at a fraction of the price of college, making student loans unnecessary. Another big benefit of modern learning is that the content can be updated much more frequently compared to any other form of education. This allows people to reduce much of the waste that comes with learning outdated material.

There are still many older individuals who don't think online education works because they themselves have a hard time learning that way. With Generation Z and beyond growing up with online education as their primary source of learning, it has become nearly unimaginable for them to learn without it. This new way of learning affects everything from K-12, career education, and every imaginable subject of interest. As time goes on and this new generation gets a bigger foothold into the workforce, the value people place on using modern learning techniques will increase.

4. Rapid Testing. The fourth fundamental concept of the lean career is to test the career in the real world as quickly as possible. This career testing, which could be in the form of an internship, apprenticeship, or entry-level position, should be very similar to what the job would be like for permanent employees. This will give an accurate representation of whether or not the career would be a good fit. Rapidly testing if a career is a good fit allows for a large reduction in wasted time and money versus deciding that it wasn't a good fit after obtaining the education. This savings in time and money allows for someone to be able to afford to test out multiple careers until they find one they want to expand on. This rapid testing also allows someone to quickly get real-world work experience, which for many companies, is the most important thing they look for in entry-level candidates. This makes transitioning into a permanent employee much easier.

I've seen countless individuals who have a skewed perception of a career due to not having any actual experience in it, but instead, only having learned about it in a classroom. If they are one of the lucky people who are able to get a job in their field after graduation, then there is a good chance they will find that their perception of what it would be like is much different from reality. This leads them to feel stuck since they took out massive amounts of student loans or feeling like they wasted years of resources on school. This feeling of being stuck is likely what causes physicians to have such a high suicide rate. Imagine someone spending over eight years of their life in school while racking up over $200,000 in student loans. They struggle with the stress and finally are able to start working in a practice only to learn that they hate their work. They seem to be out of options as they need to pay off these loans and being around the age of 30 they might even have a family that's counting on them. Their only viable option is to work for 10+ years counting the days as they slowly pay down their debt. Much of this risk could have been avoided by getting real-world experience early on while still having enough resources to change careers if it turned out to not be a great fit.

5. Just in Time Education. The last fundamental concept of the lean career is to only learn what you need to know at the time you need to know it. This gives someone an approach to broadening their career education after they've broken into a career through their specialized education. By doing this, they will rise in the ranks and advance their career through lifelong learning. This just in time education allows for maximum educational efficiency. This is due to only learning new things when they are able to use them thus reducing all the educational waste that someone would incur if they learn about a subject only to never use it and have it erode away over time.

This concept of just in time also comes from manufacturing, where Toyota learned they could reduce waste if they ordered materials from suppliers so they arrived the moment they needed them, instead of having them on hand and storing all the materials themselves. This allowed them to eliminate much of the waste that could occur if products in storage got damaged, had defects, or were never used. It also reduced the amount of labor and infrastructure needed to operate warehouses to store the materials while freeing up the financial resources they would have had invested in their inventory. They often call this the pull vs. push strategy. Instead of trying to push their inventory on the market, they let the market pull what inventory they needed at the time. For just in time to work for Toyota, they needed to have very reliable suppliers that could consistently provide new inventory at the time it was needed.

The pull vs. push strategy for education is to let the market dictate your educational needs instead of trying to push your education on the market. This strategy is the same as starting with the end goal first. Don't start with the education and then search for a role where it can be used. This is trying to push the education on the market. Instead, start with the role and let it pull what education is required to start and advance the career at the time. The key that allows just in time to work for education is the internet. It acts as our external supplier that we can order information from at the exact moment we need it, thus eliminating the need to store it internally ourselves. This just in time strategy for education, is especially useful for eliminating waste since knowledge deteriorates over time. To utilize just in time education, it is important to focus on developing self-education skills to have a reliable process to pull in information at a moment's notice.

Before the internet matured, it wasn't possible to use this just in time strategy for education. You couldn't tell your boss you need to take off work for a few months to go to a college class to learn a new skill, and you couldn't have answers to facts in just a few seconds either. This is why, in the past, it made sense to cram in as much information as you could learn in four years.

The Formula

These five fundamental concepts were put together to form a new model that creates an extremely efficient and effective way to start a great career. The four steps to this model are: identify, learn, test, and expand.

The first three steps create a cycle to rapidly get real-world experience in the role one hypothesizes would be a good fit. This allows one to see what the career is actually like and if it aligns with what they're looking for. After testing the role, they can choose to continue with it and go onto the last step, which is expand. Or they can decide to test a different career, and they repeat the rapid identify, learn, and test cycle. By using this rapid cycle, it allows them to quickly and efficiently figure out what role they want to turn into a career. Each of the following chapters will go in-depth into how you can start a great career for yourself.

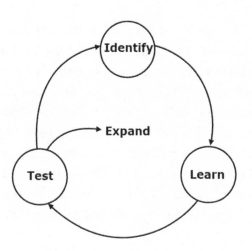

5

Identify

How many 18-year-olds do you know that are already sure about what they want to do as a career? I bet it is hard for many people to even think of one person. Identify is the first step in the lean career model. This step helps you find a career that you hypothesize would be a good fit to put through the testing cycle. This step will prove to be one of the most important as the career you identify will require a substantial commitment of time and effort. The central fundamental concept involved in this step is career as the goal. This is what will allow you to not be a drifter without a purpose, but instead give you a direction to go after.

Aligning Goals, Skills, and Interests

There are three main factors for helping identify the right career. These are your goals, skills, and interests. Being able to align these factors is what will allow you to identify a great career for yourself.

1. Goals. The most crucial factor to start with are your goals. If you don't already know precisely what you want to do, then the way to go about identifying the right career to start testing is by first thinking about your life goals. Starting with your life goals first is the most important since it's your overarching reason to even get a job in the first place. These life goals are simply the main things you want out of life. This could mean a big family, living in the country, changing the world, traveling, or whatever it is you think is important to you. To help figure out your life goals start by asking yourself questions like these:

- What is important for me to achieve in my lifetime?
- Is having a family important?
- Where do I derive most of my happiness?
- If I have only ten more years to live, then what would I do?
- When I'm lying on my deathbed at 80 years old, what would I regret not doing?

Once you figure out what you want out of life, then work backward to figure out what you need out of a career to achieve those life goals. These will be called your career goals. These goals could be things such as working in an office vs. outside, how much money you need to make, accomplishments, or perhaps flexibility to take time off. The important thing is to be realistic with what you want out of life and what kind of career it is going to take to achieve those goals. I recommend you really take the time to think hard about what it is you want out of life. Even doing things like drawing a picture of your ideal life or writing a story about yourself could prove to clear up what it is you want. After all, we only have so much time to do the things we want, so it's important to have your priorities in order. We can't do everything. To help figure out what your career goals are, start by asking yourself these questions:

- What do I really need out of a career?
- What should the work-life balance look like?
- What should the work environment look like?
- How much responsibility do I want to have?
- What do I want to accomplish in my career?
- How much money do I want to make?

By asking yourself these questions, it will allow you to really think about what kind of a career it will take to meet your life goals. If you want to have a family and spend lots of time with them, then perhaps a big part of your career aspirations should focus on work-life balance. If you aspire to be the boss, then you should realize that you will have to sacrifice much of that work-life balance to have that additional responsibility. It's tough and perhaps even unrealistic to expect to have the best of everything, so prioritizing which parts are the most important will allow you to figure out what you're willing to be flexible on in order to attain these parts of your goals.

A good example of this is if someone wants to be a high-profile lawyer, then they should first think about if it aligns with their career goals. To become a high-profile lawyer, you would have to get a formal education for seven-plus years, making you stay in school until you're at least 25. Then it is likely you will have large amounts of student loans, which makes you committed for at least another five years until you can pay it off. You may also not have much money during this period which will make starting a family or traveling more difficult. You can also expect to be working alone in an office environment for long hours every day. While these may be negatives, the positives are that you can make great money and carry great status as a lawyer. For many people, this doesn't sound appealing, but for others, it is well worth it.

Another example would be someone whose life goals are to make discoveries and ultimately win the Nobel Prize. Since these are the most important things they want out of life, their career goals should focus on learning new things, doing research, and sharing their ideas. A career that would be a perfect fit for something like this would probably involve doing research for a university or working for the government.

I met a woman named Sarah while I was in Costa Rica that loved what she was doing. She worked on an offshore oil rig which consisted of very long hours for two weeks on, and then she got two weeks off. The second two weeks were still paid, and she used that time to travel to new places all around the world. The most important thing she wanted in life was to travel, and she felt like she had cheated the system because of how well things worked out for her. This is because her life goals were aligned with her career. If Sarah instead had wanted to have a big family in the city, then I don't think her work would be such a great fit.

I also know many women whose life goal is to raise a family and spend most of their time at home with them. These women's career goals to be able to accomplish this probably won't put too much emphasis on long term career trajectory, or big career accomplishments. They instead will put a high priority on flexibility or work-life balance while just being able to make sufficient money. Many of these women have found that being a teacher fits their career goals perfectly. They only need four years of schooling, which means less student loans. They make enough money to live on or provide supplemental income for the family. They also have an amazing work-life balance and are flexible enough to find work elsewhere if they need to move. I believe this is one of the main reasons the majority of teachers are women.

There is a guy who had a good government job making over $80,000 a year. He ended up quitting it after 11 years to work in a supermarket part-time. He's realized he wasn't happy in his current job and didn't want to work in an office environment anymore. He didn't really need the money either since he realized his ideal life didn't require that much. He talked about how much happier he is now since he's living a much simpler life that helped reduce his stress. He also has more time to spend with his relatives, which is important to him. This isn't an isolated case, either. I've met countless people just like this guy who left their seemingly good jobs for something much different and are happier because of it. Some people have moved overseas to work remote while others have moved out of the city to be in the country.

Everyone is different. For me, my life goals are very focused on accomplishment and having an impact on the world. I also get bored very easily and find the challenges of life fulfilling. I've found that if I'm not accomplishing things or making progress, then I feel dissatisfied. My career goals would prioritize things such as long-term career trajectory, responsibility, learning, and working long hours. This type of career is where I will be most happy. Gary Vaynerchuk, who's an entrepreneur and social media influencer, has a personality very similar to mine. His happiness is derived from his accomplishments. Gary often talks about how he knows of people who are happy making $40,000 a year and being the little league coach for their kids' baseball team, but he also knows he could never be happy doing that.

After talking to many 16-20-year-olds, I've learned that for the majority of them, their main goal is focused on just being able to move out and support themselves comfortably. If you have a hard time thinking any further than a short-term goal like this, then that's completely normal. You don't have to have some huge goal or plan for your life at such a young age. Just go after your goal and accomplish it. The more goals you accomplish, the more you will learn about yourself and figure out what your next goal to go after will be. Over time you will learn more about what you want until you can form an overarching vision of the most important things you want out of life. At the end of the day, everyone has different goals and things that make them feel happy and fulfilled. It's your job to work on figuring out what those are so you can design your life around them. Don't be discouraged if you don't know exactly what those things are right away. Life goals are not static. They change. New circumstances or discoveries about yourself will alter what you want out of life and gives you new things to chase. This is what keeps life interesting.

2. Skills. After you think you figured out what your career goals are, the next step is to look at your skills. Think about your soft skills and inherent personality. These are the types of things that you seem to be naturally better at. Are you more of an analytical person that likes to be alone, or are you a very outgoing person that loves talking? Are you more of a doer or more of a thinker? You might want to take one or more personality tests to help you figure it out. You can start by searching for "best career assessment personality test." This will help determine the types of work you would be best suited for. Some personalities will be better in certain roles than others. For example, I learned I am a very extroverted person and would have a very hard time working in a role where I was alone and didn't talk to others. You can also think about what you were naturally good at and enjoyed in high school. Were you good at writing or math? Knowing these things are very important since it will determine the roles in which your skills can really shine.

You also want to be thinking about where you can add the most value that others can't. These are your unique skills and abilities that you're extremely strong in. The people that find a way to apply their gifts are often considered a prodigy. A good example of this would be Santiago Gonzalez, who learned very early on his personality was a great fit for programming. He got very good at computer programming, and by age 16 he was on track to finish a master's degree in computer science. If he didn't take advantage of his inherent strengths in programming and instead tried to improve his weaknesses in communication, then he wouldn't be a prodigy. He wouldn't be able to add nearly as much value to the world if he didn't focus on his unique strengths.

Jeff Bezos is a good example of someone who figured out what area they were not strong in. Jeff wanted to be a theoretical physicist and went to Princeton University to study. He did very well in school and got A+ grades while being in the honors physics track. He told a story of how he was in a quantum mechanics class and couldn't solve a partial differential equation. He spent three hours trying to solve one homework problem and still couldn't find the answer. He thought of someone else in the class who was the best physicist he knew. After showing him the problem, he just stared at it and came up with the correct answer. Jeff said that was the very moment he realized he was never going to be a great theoretical physicist. This is because Jeff wanted to be the best at whatever he did and if he couldn't be the best theoretical physicist, then at least he learned sooner than later. We can now thank him for finding a way to use his unique skills and abilities for creating what Amazon is today.

3. Interests. The last part of this analysis is to determine your interests. Your interests are what you enjoy doing or learning about for fun. Do you like computers? Do you like cars? There are probably lots of things you are drawn to. This will help determine the type of company and industry you're best suited for. Some roles are also industry-specific, so this can be very important. You know it's a strong interest if you would be doing these things even if you weren't getting paid. These interests are often referred to as passions. I firmly believe it is not always smart to follow your passion as a career. Imagine someone whose passion is singing and does everything they can do become a singer. The only problem is that they have a terrible voice and can't sing. For example, some people go on American Idol because their passion is singing; however, they find out they are not as good as they thought they were.

A career involves making money; however, many passions people have do not have the ability to earn money or even come close to meeting their career goals. This means their passion would be better classified as a hobby. Mike Rowe is one of the best people to talk to about this subject. He has met and talked to more people that have a passion for doing jobs that they couldn't have possibly had a passion for doing before they started doing it. For example, he met a guy who became a multi-millionaire from his septic tank cleaning business. He said, "I looked around to see where everyone was headed, then I went the opposite way. Then I got good at my work. Then I began to prosper. Then one day, I realized I was passionate about other people's crap." The reason for this is because passions grow with success and praise just as they diminish with failure and criticism. Try to remember how your passions started in the first place. You can probably think back to a time when you just started doing it, and it was only slightly interesting to you. As you began to do it more and more, then it became a bigger part of your life. You began to get good at it and take pride in it. People began to associate you with this new thing, and it became part of your identity. This is how passions are created.

Most likely, the people who turn their work into their passion also meet their career goals. Think about it. If someone works outside for 12 hours a day, but their life goals involve working in a 9-5 office job, then they probably wouldn't be very happy. If someone isn't happy, it would be hard for them to turn their work into a passion. Also, if they were not good at the job because their skill set wasn't a match, then they wouldn't take pride in their work or get praised for it. This too, would make it very unlikely that they would be able to turn their work into their passion.

Something interesting happens when you start with your goals and skills first while building the passion along the way. This process of building your passion takes many hours in which you are continuously learning more about the work and improving your skills until you reach a point of mastery. At the start, it might seem hard to stick with it while you're still not the best. As time goes on and you improve, then you will find it easier to work longer and harder. Once you take pride in your work and it becomes a part of your identity, then you will realize it's your passion. The people who build their passions this way are also the ones who are able to build their own businesses around them or become the top people in organizations. This is due to the work ethic that seems to come much easier to people who have a passion for their work and the immense number of hours someone has put in the industry to reach the point of mastery where they can think much more creatively about it. As time goes on the person who built the passion along the way seems to only be getting happier and doing better in their career.

On the contrary, if someone were to start with their passion first, things might not work out as well. The person who starts with their passion will probably be much happier at the start since they feel like they're doing what they love. The problems start when overtime they come to realize that their passion as a career doesn't fulfill the life goals that are so important to them. They might also realize that their skillset isn't as good of a match as they thought for the type of work they are doing. They begin to constantly feel like they aren't good enough and start to resent it. They don't enjoy doing it anymore, and their work ethic goes down. They then get criticized for not doing a good job, and they definitely don't want to talk about it after work. What once was their passion is no longer something they take pride in or associate their identity with. As time goes on the person who built their career starting from their passion only seems to be getting unhappier and doing worse in their career. This is with the few exceptions where someone's passion actually turns out to match their career goals and align with their skills. For all the people you hear who say follow your passion, they often built their passion along the way but forgot to mention that part.

Opportunity

What is opportunity? An opportunity is just identifying a way you can use your abilities to fulfill a market need that allows you to meet your goals or at least get closer to your goals. The important part to note that many people miss is that you must find a way to fulfill a market need. Without that market need your opportunity is no more than a hobby since you won't be able to make money from it. Mike Rowe also talked about opportunities like this. "People I've met on my journeys, by and large, didn't realize their dream. They looked around for an opportunity. They identified the opportunity, they exploited the opportunity, they worked at the opportunity, and then they got good at the opportunity. And then they figured out how to love it."

The Bullseye

How do you go about identifying the right career based on your goals, skills, and interests? I've come up with a simple chart to help align these three factors to identify the most promising careers. I call this chart the bullseye. Most people try a variety of things such as traveling, going to college, and getting different entry-level jobs to hopefully figure out what they want to do for a career. With the bullseye, you now have a model you can follow, so you know you're on the right path to finding a great career. You will not be one of the many people that take the path of least resistance and stays at whatever job you can keep. Even if you think you already know what you want to do, I highly suggest you go through this exercise. It could bring some great careers to the surface that you never even thought about before. The bullseye is a chart that consists of three rings.

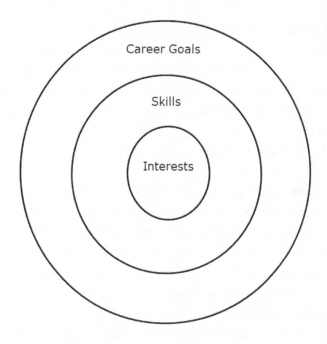

1. Career Goals. This is your starting point for identifying which careers might be a good fit. Your career goals are the broadest and fundamental reasons a career will either be a hit or miss. This is why it's so important to start with a career that at least meets your most core goals. The way to use this chart is by listing out all the different careers you can think of that meet your career goals in this outer ring. There isn't any limit on the number of careers you can list here. You should strive to have at least ten, but the more you have listed is better. This will probably require you to do some initial research into different careers to be able to create a big enough list to start from. You can use websites that list out different careers such as careerplanner.com/listofcareers.cfm to help you build out your list. When you are doing research into each career, you should try to learn the basics to see if you think they will meet your career goals or not. These careers that you list out should also be the entry-level jobs you would start at. This means that even if you want to be a movie director or sales executive, you need to work backward to figure out which entry-level roles you could start at to eventually get there. You can then research all these entry-level roles to see if they match your career goals. If they do, then add them to your bullseye.

2. Skills. Skills are second because you are only allowed to pick careers that are in your career goals ring. This allows you to further shortlist which careers are the best fit for you. What you'll do here is look at all the careers that are in your career goals ring and pick the ones that best align with your skills. You can choose up to six different careers for this ring. This is where you should try to cross-examine which roles your personality and unique skill set would best be served. During this exercise, try to think objectively about how it fits in with your skillset. Subjecting your opinions about previous preconceptions of different careers might only cause you to miss the perfect opportunity. Keep in mind that the best opportunities are often the careers that aren't so popular making the demand higher than the supply.

3. Interests. This is where you will look at all the careers you have in your skills ring and pick up to three that interest you the most. The reason this is last is because interests fluctuate much more than your fundamental career goals or natural skills do. It makes much more sense to start with them first, then see if by chance one of these careers also is a passion of yours. If not already a passion, then building a passion around one shouldn't be too hard. These interests could be on things you already know about or on things you would like to know more about. A career could interest you because of its economics, such as supply/demand or market value. It could also be because of the long-term growth of the industry or how this career aligns with your overall vision. It could be really anything about a career that makes you intrigued to learn more. If none of the careers interest you, then just list out the top three you would choose if you had to pick.

Once you finished your bullseye, the next step is to do a much more in-depth analysis of the three careers in your inner circle. This in-depth analysis should include everything from what a day in the life of the career looks like, to career growth, industry growth, etc. Since whichever career you choose to test will take a significant commitment of your resources, it's important to invest enough time upfront in research, so you feel confident in whichever career you choose. This confidence in your decision is what will make you stick with a career when the learning becomes difficult or getting your foot in the door seems impossible. Once you've thoroughly researched all three of these careers, then you will need to pick the most promising one to test. This choice is nothing more than a hypothesis that this will be a great career for you. As with all hypotheses, the only way to prove them is to test them. Without testing it, there is really no way to be entirely sure about it. If you feel that none of the three careers you researched are a good fit for you, then you can do this exercise again by adding more careers to your goals ring and narrowing it down.

The ultimate goal of the lean career is to quickly as possible get real-world experience. This means that even if a career turns out to not be something you want to stick with you still have the resources to test another career, but this time with the knowledge you gained about what you liked or disliked from your previous test making it much more likely for the next test to strike home. With just a few testing cycles, most people would have learned so much about themselves and what they want out of a career that it would be hard to not find a great career for themselves. You will also gain an immense amount of transferable skills which will make your next test considerably easier while also making you more valuable to employers. During these testing cycles, you might even learn about different careers you never even considered and develop a new interest.

A fictional example of someone using this bullseye chart to identify a great career will be Mike. Mike is an 18-year-old who just graduated high school, and his overall career vision is to work in a stable job that pays enough to support a family while living in a suburb of a city within five years. Mike doesn't care about being the boss and instead prioritizes work-life balance. Short term he wants to be able to afford to support himself which would require him to make at least $40,000 a year. He doesn't want to go to college so the career must not be regulated to require a degree, and he must be able to learn it outside of college. This allows Mike to think about every type of career that fits within his career goals. He considers everything, from different business roles such as IT, technology, sales, and marketing, to the different trades in construction and even careers in logistics. Mike spends a couple of days researching all these different careers and now has a list of about 20 different entry-level roles across all these industries that fit his career goals.

Mike then goes onto the next ring of the bullseye and needs to identify the top 6 careers that are best aligned with his skill set. Mike knows that he is much more introverted and isn't the best at communicating with people. He would do best in a role where he works alone or with a small team. Mike also recalls that during high school, he was much better in his technical classes such as science, math, robotics, and programming. This allows Mike to identify six different careers in the areas of IT, engineering, and data analytics. Mike then goes onto the final ring of the bullseye and needs to identify the top three careers that are best aligned with his interests. Mike knows he is much more interested in using technology than he is in actually creating it. This makes him lean more towards IT and data analytics than engineering. Mike realizes he is also interested in doing analysis. Mike chooses his top three careers as follows. Data analyst, marketing analyst, and database administrator.

Mike now has to choose which one of these three he is going to choose for his test. He is first going to spend a couple of hours researching each one of these to see if he uncovers anything else that might help influence his decision. This could be any information that changes his assumptions of a career or just makes him more interested in it. After doing in-depth research into each career, Mike realizes that the marketing analyst career really interests him. It seems to be a more entry-level position, and he should be able to learn everything he needs online and relatively quickly. This would allow him to meet his goal of being able to move out and live on his own in less than a year. He also finds it rewarding to see how much money he makes his company based on the improved marketing from his analysis. On top of that, there is also a big demand for people that are skilled in this role, and it isn't taught in college, which makes it easier to get your foot in the door. This is the career Mike hypothesizes will be a great career for him and decides to put it through the testing cycle.

There are some people out there who will suggest starting with learning a skill. While this strategy does work, it is still much smarter to start with the career first instead of the skill. This is because learning a specific skill doesn't always mean a person will be able to make money from it. Even if they enjoy the skill and are good at it, the position that they might be able to obtain from their expertise could involve many other aspects that they aren't as good at or don't like doing.

Another problem is starting with the company first instead of the role. This is like someone deciding they want to work at Google or any other company they think is great. This strategy isn't the best either since to be valuable to a company a person needs to have that specialized skill set required to do the role they were hired for. This would make it very hard for them to get hired at their dream company since they likely don't have a skill set that the company values. If they were to somehow get hired at the company only to learn they had to do a role that they weren't good at and perhaps even hated, then the 40 hours a week spent at the job would not be worth the benefits of being able to work at their ideal company.

Finding an Entry Point

Do you have a career in mind, but don't know where to start to be able to get your foot in the door? Many people will think about careers that aren't the starting point since that's what they read about or know about from others. For many of these careers, there are multiple paths that lead to them. This means that if you identify a career that seems to be a great fit only to learn that it's not an entry-level position, then you will need to decide which entry point you will take to break into that career.

Starting with a career that requires multiple steps isn't a bad thing, though. It will often motivate you to push through difficulties until you reach your career goal. Think about the smartest people you knew in high school who always worked harder than everyone else. Most likely, most of them were not much smarter than everyone else, but instead, they just worked harder since they had a goal which required them to do well in school. This goal could have been to get into a great college or perhaps become a doctor. This was the driving force of their motivation. Over time the people that will actually reach their goal learned to enjoy the process of getting their and took pride in it. These are the people who are willing to put in the extra hours to study since they know it's getting them closer to reaching their goal and enjoy showing off their academic achievement.

Imagine someone whose goal was to become a doctor, but hated school because they constantly struggled to make good grades. They never learned to enjoy school, nor did they take pride in it. This person would have a very hard time becoming a doctor because they were never able to enjoy the process of getting there. If this person instead started with the goal of going through medical school, then they might have come to the realization much sooner that becoming a doctor might not be the best fit for them.

To be able to successfully achieve a career which requires multiple steps, you must enjoy the process of getting there, whether that is the required education or the entry-level roles you have to succeed in. In many of these entry-level roles, you will need to work very hard and become very good at in order to get promoted. This is why it is critical to only use entry-level roles in your bullseye chart. You can then use your ultimate career goal as the deciding factor to pick which role to test in your interests' ring.

What if you want to find an entry point into a career that is regulated by the government? First, you should find an entry point into a role where you can do similar work without going to college or at least work closely with someone who is in the career you want. By doing this, it will allow you to greatly reduce the risk of going through all the required schooling to only learn that you don't enjoy the actual work. There are so many cases of people going to school to become a lawyer or doctor with a misconceived perception of the job only to learn it's something they don't want to do after spending so much time and money. If you identify a career that is regulated to require extensive schooling or a certification, you should search for every related entry-level job that doesn't require the schooling or certification. This could be an adjacent role that isn't regulated, an internship, an apprenticeship, or just shadowing someone working in the field. This entry-level job will help you learn more about what the career would be like if you continued with the education and certification.

An example of this could be someone whose career they identified on their bullseye was to become a lawyer. With it being a regulated career, it might seem like the only way to know if they want to do it is by going through the schooling, passing the bar, and getting an entry-level position. Instead of going through that whole process and risk not enjoying being a lawyer, this person instead identifies every position they could do to work closely with lawyers. This reduces the risk of choosing the wrong career before going down this long path.

Which Careers are Hot?

When identifying which careers are right for you, it's important to consider how it will be affected by the market demand. This market demand has huge impacts on nearly all aspects of a career's opportunity, which could be the deciding factors if a career will meet your goals or not. It affects how hard a career will be to break into, how much money you will make, and the rate at which you're promoted. After all, opportunities are all about aligning your goals, skills, and interests with a real market need that creates value for people.

1. Breaking into a career. This is a very important factor to consider since if you can't get your foot in the door, you will have no choice but to choose a different career. You also have to consider how much time it will take to land that first position once you start your search. If it is going to take months, then you better have enough money saved to last that long while also having the mental strength to push through the seemingly constant rejection of your application. Supply and Demand is the basis of our economy, and the way it impacts the difficulty of breaking into a career is no exception. If there is a low demand of employers hiring for a position, yet a high supply of people trying to get the position, then it will be much harder to break in. You will be competing with many other people for only a few available positions making it very difficult to differentiate yourself from all the others. A good example of this that I mentioned in a previous chapter is the discrepancy between the number of people majoring in Anthropology and the number of jobs available making it about a one in five hundred chance of someone with an anthropology degree actually breaking into the field.

I also know a few people who are going to college for criminal justice because they want to be an FBI agent. The problem is that there are over 130,000 people that graduate with criminal justice degrees every year. After looking at a list of jobs for US citizens on fbijobs.gov, I was only able to find 15 open positions. Out of the 15, it looked like well over half of them required a particular skill set in IT or finance making criminal justice majors unqualified. This means that if someone wants to break into the FBI by becoming a criminal justice major, they have to compete for around five positions with 130,000 other people who may have gone to better schools, have more experience, and have inside connections.

While a career that is hard to break into will be very competitive and require lots of grit, it can also be very rewarding. Venture capital is a good example of a career that is extremely hard to break into directly out of school, but if you do, you are on a fast track to lots of high paying opportunities that people without your experience wouldn't have access to. The reason it's so hard to break into is because firms don't need to hire that many people and the type of education required to do this work is very difficult to learn. The work you do is also extremely high value as the decisions you make could easily have a multi-million-dollar impact on the firm. This is what attracts the smartest and most motivated people to venture capital while also inevitably making it a very competitive career to break into. If you're up for the challenge, then don't shy away from something just because it has a high barrier to entry. After all, if it was easy, then everyone would do it.

2. How much money you make. This factor is very dependent on your career goals, which will determine the type of life you can afford to live. Supply and Demand also have the most significant impact on the amount of money a career will pay. I talked about this quite a bit in chapter 3, where I reference why careers such as computer programming pay so much compared to many other engineering fields. It all comes down to the huge demand employers have for this role and the supply not meeting that demand causing employers to increase wages to be able to compete for talent. This supply and demand can be impacted by things such as government regulation, difficulty, and willingness to actually do the job. In some cases, there are great jobs available that people don't even know about, which is why the supply is so low.

The market value of a job is the second major piece which determines how much a career pays. The reason the venture capital role I mentioned above pays so well is due to the monetary impact a single person's decision can make. This makes that person's role have a very high value and makes sense to pay whatever it takes to get the best talent. Another example I mentioned on this in chapter 3 was how just 100 people working on an oil rig could impact billions in revenue, making each employee highly valued no matter how simple the job might be.

3. The rate at which you are promoted. This factor is very important for people whose career goal entails them rising up in the ranks or becoming the boss. If your ultimate career goal requires multiple promotions to get there, then knowing the rate at which different paths get promoted to that career could be of the utmost importance to you. Demand for a position is probably the biggest driver of how fast a certain career is promoted. The more people a company is hiring for a position, the easier it is for those already in it to be promoted to more senior or management roles.

A good example of this is sales vs. marketing. If a company is hiring ten people in their sales department for every one person in their marketing department, then the people in sales will get promoted much faster. Many companies do most of their hiring at the entry-level, which means they will need to promote from within to fill the more senior positions. There will also be opportunities to become a manager of these new entry-level people. I've seen salespeople work their way up from the bottom to a leadership position in just a matter of a few years due to a rapidly growing sales team. On the other hand, in roles like marketing where they don't hire nearly as many people, it will often take much longer for positions to open up. This is simply due to there not being as many people in the department.

If you're in an industry that is only comprised of a few people on the team, then you should recognize that it could be years before you get a promotion. I've heard of cases where the only way someone gets a promotion is if their boss leaves and this could have someone waiting for many years. Understanding this is very important for long term career trajectory. The type of company you pick also has a big impact on your rate of promotion. If the company has a very large department in your field, then you will likely have more promotion opportunities compared to another company whose department is very small. If the company is growing the department fast, then that will also give you many opportunities to move up if the company is known for hiring from within. There are many factors you will learn to assess once you have a clear career goal to go after.

6

Learn

The second step, once you've identified a career you would like to test is to learn about it. The two fundamental concepts that come into play here are specializing first and modern learning. This learning process is what allows you to differentiate yourself to employers with your relevant and valuable knowledge. It also shows you how to remove much of the bloat in education, thus saving you large amounts of time and money.

Minimum Viable Knowledge

Minimum viable knowledge, also referred to as MVK, is the most important principle to understand in this chapter. MVK is the least amount of knowledge that is required to accurately test the career you've chosen. This idea was first taken from Eric Ries' book, The Lean Startup, where he talks about the minimum viable product. Eric learned that the first goal of any startup is to quickly as possible create a product that would allow entrepreneurs to test their assumptions about a business. The best way to do this was to create the simplest product possible to accomplish this test as anything more you create would just be wasted if your assumptions were wrong. Once you choose a career entry-point, this same idea can be applied to education which allows you to quickly as possible test what the career is actually like in the real world using only the minimal amount of education. If you were to learn more than what was minimally required for the job and then realize you don't enjoy the work after testing it in the real world, then that extra education would have been wasted. Therefore, for the career you have chosen, you should specialize your education to only learn the minimal amount required to be able to get a job or internship and do the job effectively. This minimal amount of knowledge is strongly correlated to the minimum amount that's required to be valuable to a company.

There are some careers with entry points that do not require any learning to be able to get real-world work experience. Some examples of careers like this are in the skilled trades or construction as an apprentice or a laborer. This is because basic labor is valuable without any education. If you can start getting real work experience from day one, then do that. This work experience, even if low skill, will allow you to work alongside others in more skilled roles giving you insight into what the career is actually like. It will also give you more context and real-world application when learning higher-skilled work. If you want a career in construction management and had construction experience, then the class material would be much easier to grasp since you have real-world context to compare the education to.

On the other end of the spectrum, there are careers that could take months of learning to get real-world work experience. This is usually due to the entry-level job requiring a very high skill level or competition with college students or graduates. This is where your specialized education, in which you acquired job-specific skills, will differentiate you from the competition. Some examples of careers that have a high skill level would be in technical roles such as programming or IT. These types of careers often require people to have skills that could take months or perhaps even years to acquire before becoming valuable enough to be hired in even an internship. Other office type roles such as sales or human resources are often filled with lots of competition from college graduates even though they might not require much skill to break into. These types of roles are where you will have to use your relevant and valuable education in the career to stand out from all the college graduates that have limited knowledge of the skills required to do the job.

One of the careers I tested out when trying to find one that was a great fit for me was welding. Instead of trying to learn how to weld, I was able to find a job as an apprentice where I would do all the nonskilled manual labor alongside a welder. This allowed me to very quickly get real-world experience working with a welder and seeing what the job is actually like. It didn't take more than two weeks to learn that being a welder wasn't for me. By getting that experience very quickly, it eliminated all the waste that would have occurred if I spent loads of time and money trying to learn how to weld to only find out it wasn't what I wanted to do.

The other career I tested after welding was sales development. I could get work experience in welding with no experience, but that definitely wasn't the case with sales development. I was competing with other people who had either a college degree or more sales experience than me. This meant I was going to have to invest more in the learning portion. It took about one month to learn all the basics of sales development. I already had good communication and interpersonal skills that I had been practicing for a couple years. This one month of specialized knowledge in the role is what allowed me to stand out from the others who were seemingly more qualified.

The main takeaway from this section is that your ultimate goal is to get into a role where you can get real-world experience. Once you get into a role where you are working alongside others in the industry, you will have great people to be your mentors and give you guidance. Just by being around them, you will find yourself continually learning from them. Your new job is your testing ground where you should apply everything you learned and continue with on the job learning. You will see how learning has a direct impact on improving your work, which should keep you motivated.

One thing to be aware of is if you don't learn enough to do the job effectively and can't handle the work; it could cause you enough stress to make you not enjoy the job. It's important to understand how much you need to know to do the job effectively and your tolerance for stress. If you easily break under stress, then it's advisable to over-prepare with the education, so you aren't too stressed out having to quickly learn on the job. This could cause you to quit prematurely and change careers even if you would have enjoyed it. If you can handle stress, then you would probably do fine getting into a role a little over your head where you need to learn quickly to be successful. After all, pressure makes diamonds. I've talked to many people who went into a role where at first, they struggled, but they pushed through the hardship and started getting better. They took pride in conquering this obstacle and continued to improve until they were great at it. Don't be afraid if you aren't good at something initially. Push through the difficulty and improve. Knowing when to push through vs. change is more of an art than a science.

What to Learn

Now that you understand the goal of learning is to get the
MVK, the next step is to figure out the three different parts that
make up the outline for this minimum viable knowledge.

1. Soft skills are the first part of the outline as they serve as
the fundamental requirements to be successful in a career.
These skills are ones that can be observed, such as
communication skills, organizational skills, and being detail
oriented. Hopefully, you already picked a career that aligns
with your soft skills and natural personality. It's very hard to
change your soft skills. That would be like changing your
entire personality since certain personalities typically come
with a set of soft skills or traits. For example, people that are
introverted and have good analytical and detail-oriented skills
are less likely to have good communication and interpersonal
skills.

If you end up learning that your soft skills are not aligned
with the career you've chosen, then you should really question
if this is the right career for you. As an example, if someone
thought about being a paid advertisement marketing associate,
but they learned it requires a much more analytical personality
than they originally thought, then they should probably
reconsider that career. This person knows that analytics is not
one of their strengths, nor do they care about improving it. It
would be smart of this person to consider picking another
occupation that is better aligned with their skills and consider
themselves lucky to figure this out sooner than later.

If you learn that your soft skills are aligned with the career,
then you should focus on improving the ones that are the most
valuable for you to be successful in that role. As a general rule,
it is normally better to focus on improving your strengths

instead of trying to fix your weaknesses as long as your strengths are also the most valuable part of the role. Being above average in the most important skills will easily compensate for your weakness in the less valuable skills.

2. Hard skills are the second part of the outline as they serve as your greatest medium for providing value to a company in an entry-level job. These are skills you're able to prove you have without saying a word. Employers can normally give tests to see if you have these types of skills. Some examples include computer literacy, knowing how to use a program, or how to execute a process. In the trades, these hard skills could be things such as welding or plumbing. The majority of entry-level jobs that pay well will normally require very specific hard skills. This is because most entry-level jobs consist of only executing a process utilizing different hard skills designed by someone much more senior. Generally, the more specific and difficult the skill, the less supply of talent there is, which causes the pay to go up. If your soft skills are aligned with the role, then acquiring the hard skills should come much easier even if you have no previous experience with a skill.

3. Knowledge is the last part of the outline as it serves as a great way to differentiate yourself by showing your interest in a particular field or industry. This knowledge is your expertise on a subject. It's your ability to have a conversation around it. It could be everything from theoretical knowledge of how something works to industry knowledge and lingo. An example of knowledge for computer programming would be your understanding of the theoretical aspects of computer science and why programs work vs. knowing how to program in Java.

Without knowledge or understanding the fundamentals of what makes something work, it's virtually impossible to problem solve or come up with new ideas. Knowledge also becomes more useful as the seniority of the role increases. This is because the role requires a fundamental understanding of a field and industry to be able to create the processes and strategies for the entry-level workers to execute. Knowledge is also the driving factor in promotions since you need to thoroughly understand all aspects of a job to be able to get promoted to manage others.

The Outline

You must understand what you need to learn, so you don't waste your time and money learning unnecessary things. The strategy I recommend using to figure out this MVK involves creating an outline which will serve as your plan of attack and help keep you on track.

To figure out what the MVK is for each one of the parts described above, I recommend listing out the top five in each category, starting with the most important. By only listing out the top five, it forces you to prioritize the most important things. This allows you to focus your time to reach the minimum viable knowledge faster. There are a few different ways to figure out the top five in each category. One of the best ways I've found to do this is by reading every job description you can find for the career and looking for similarities between them. If you find that they all list a certain skill, then that's probably a very important skill for that career. Some job descriptions even categorize desired soft skills, hard skills, and knowledge making it easier for you to compare to other job descriptions.

Another good way to figure out the top five in each category is to simply do research. Search for phrases such as "how to start a _____ career" or "requirements to get ____ job." Read as many articles as you can on the career or the entry-level career role while searching through forums like Reddit where people talk about their experience in that career. While doing this research, you will start to see similarities with what people say is required to break into the role. Find what seems to be the most important and common requirements then compare them to the list you already compiled from the job descriptions. Hopefully, they match up, but if they don't, replace the ones that you feel confident are the most important.

My personal favorite way to figure out the top five is by talking to people who recently started working in the field you are interested in. It's better if these people have a background similar to yours, so their experience breaking into the field will likely be more relevant to you. These similarities could be things such as education, experience, location, etc. While this technique requires you to put yourself out there, it helps you figure out the MVK much faster. The people you reach out to could also serve as mentors for your learning process, which will be talked about more later. The skills you develop by reaching out to people are also the same skills you will use in getting an internship, making it great practice.

As of 2019, LinkedIn is one of your greatest resources for utilizing this model and finding others who can help you along the way. One way to do this is by searching LinkedIn for the names of the people who wrote the articles you read from your research. These people are obviously knowledgeable and interested in the topic so they would likely be more than happy to help someone who's trying to start their career in the same field as them. Another way to find people is by searching LinkedIn and filtering by job title of the career you are interested in. You can also filter by location or education to find people with a similar background.

Once you find these people, you should connect with them on LinkedIn and send them a message about how you enjoyed the article they wrote and how you are interested in the career and was hoping they could give some advice on how to get started in it. More often than not, these people will want to help you so don't be afraid to send follow up messages or send them an email to make sure they got your message.

A good example of how I used this strategy was when I was curious about a career in logistics sales. I searched for articles on how to break into logistics sales and found a great article about it on LinkedIn. After reading the article, I searched LinkedIn for the person who wrote it. I found out he was the owner of a consulting company that provides sales training to logistics companies. His phone number was on his profile, so I gave him a call and told him how I just read his article on breaking into logistics sales and how I was interested in starting a career in it. He was happy to help and proceeded to spend an hour talking to me all about how logistics sales work and how to go about starting a career in it. He gave me information that would have taken days to compile on my own, all because I made one call.

How to Learn

Some people say they're going to college to learn how to learn, but learning doesn't happen in the classroom anymore. You need to be able to learn in our fast-changing world by improving your ability to learn online and self-educate. Being able to learn this way is the only way you will be able to stay relevant in today's economy. Companies can't send you to classes every weekend to stay up to date and being able to self-educate is quickly becoming one of the top skills companies are looking for in candidates now.

The CEO of LinkedIn, Jeff Weiner, says that when hiring, one of the biggest things he looks for is a fast learning curve. He said, "These are folks that are going to be comfortable going into a situation where they may not be expert they may not have the requisite experience, but they're capable of learning really, really fast and they not only are capable of learning, they really enjoy the process of learning--which makes it that much easier." If you for some reason are unable to learn online or without a teacher spoon-feeding you, then you should really consider going into a career that doesn't change much thus not requiring much additional learning.

How should someone go about learning? There are two main methods for learning; the traditional model for learning which is often found in K-12 and colleges, and the modern model for learning, which is often found in the real world. The traditional model for learning includes going into a large classroom where a teacher gives the class a lecture based on material in a textbook. If someone didn't understand something or had a question, then they could ask the teacher during this class time. After class, the students might have some sort of project or assignment to do to practice what they had just learned (aka homework). When doing homework, students could reference the textbook if they forgot something from class or didn't understand it. Students could also work on these assignments or study with other students.

There is also waste involved with in-person classes. This includes the time spent traveling between classes and the delay between classes, which more than often results in downtime. This is how most colleges structure how students learn, and there are still a few industries which are best served through learning with the traditional model. Industries, such as the sciences or medicine, that require the use of expensive equipment, which is only accessible in a classroom, are an excellent example of these.

The modern model for learning includes doing online research from anywhere in the world. This research includes long-form material such as books or online courses. It can also include many different types of short-form content, such as articles, videos, and podcasts. People learn at their own pace; however fast or slow that may be. The students can seek people with domain experience to serve as mentors to them to help speed up their learning curve while keeping them accountable. These students can also connect with others learning the same material to form study groups. This modern model combined with on the job training, and real-world application is by far the best education for the majority of careers.

1. Books are considered a long form learning material which could be used almost exclusively to learn an entire subject. Just like textbooks are the base for most classes in the traditional model for learning, books are also the base for modern learning. This is because books are often very comprehensive and provide the underlying fundamentals required to build on top of. It's important to first understand the fundamentals of something new you're trying to learn since, as you learned in chapter two, people rationalize new information through analogies of previously known information. The fundamentals you know give you a way to compare the new information you learn against what you know is true.

There's so much content out there that is complete trash, and that's why it's so important to start by learning the fundamentals from a reputable source. These fundamentals allow you to filter out the BS based on the truths you know. An example of this for car detailing would be to first understand the fundamentals of how removing scratches works through the use of abrasives and the fundamentals of different types of paint such as base coat vs. clear coat. This makes it much easier for the detailer to conceptualize new techniques since they can rationalize how they work by comparing it to the fundamental truths they know about detailing. They will also be able to identify which techniques are garbage and to problem solve since they know what's fundamentally required for something to work.

For bodybuilding, some of the first fundamental things to understand would be calories, macronutrients, and what makes our bodies build muscle or lose fat. By understanding these truths, it allows trainers and coaches to rationalize which workout plans or diets will work best based on someone's goals. It will also allow them to problem solve why a muscle-building routine isn't working for someone by comparing it to the truths they know about what's required to build muscle.

I remember listening to a podcast and hearing the billionaire founder of Drobox, Drew Huston, talk about the way he learned new things for his business. Whatever topic he needed to learn about he would start by finding the top three rated books about that subject and read all three of them. This was always his starting point for learning something new. Elon Musk also often credits himself being able to learn rocket science by just reading a lot of books about it.

At the start, you will want to cast a very wide net on your career education. This means reading the most general books on your career to get a full understanding of how it works. You can find which books are the best for this by searching the internet for top books for _____ career. You can also search Amazon.com for the top-rated books in ____ career. Amazon will also show you the recommended books under the top-rated books. By far, one of the best ways for figuring out which books to read is by asking for recommendations from people in the industry. I actually read my first sales fundamental book by having it recommended to me from someone I met at a tech sales gathering.

   2. Online courses are also considered a long form learning material which could be used to learn entire subjects without many other resources. While teachers give lectures to a class normally based on material in a textbook, online courses are often the same as a very well thought out lecture given by a teacher. This is a relatively new invention with most online courses being produced after 2010. These courses are also often associated with a book or would work well in parallel with a book. They can span over just a couple hours to hundreds of hours of video depending on the depth of the subject being taught. These courses could also supplement books as a base if they are comprehensive enough to teach the fundamentals. Some subjects are taught best with online courses because the video can help people learn more through visuals.

   Khan Academy has effectively used online courses to help teach many different K-12 subjects that have proven to be learned better through video compared to a textbook. Again, you will want to cast a wide net with the online courses and learn as much stuff as you can about the career you've chosen. You can search for lists of top online courses for ___ career. I've found that one of the best ways to go about finding these online courses is by searching the different platforms that provide them such as Coursera, Udemy, EdX, Etc.

   3. Articles, videos, and podcasts are considered short form learning material. These resources are great for cherry-picking bits of information about a topic or going in-depth on something specific. These resources should be used to support long-form material. If there are any topics you don't understand or want to learn more about, then these short-form materials are perfect for that. These can normally be found with a simple search about the topic you're interested in. For more scientific topics, these materials could be research papers or different studies.

4. Mentors are great resources for giving guidance, keeping you accountable and they play a very similar role to what a traditional teacher does. They provide interaction to help answer any questions you have about a topic and give you guidance about different things to learn. Just like teachers, they also help keep you accountable to continue progressing. Learning from mentors can be through a live video, a phone call, or in person. Normally the more advanced learners understand the importance of mentors and just how quickly a great one can accelerate your learning curve.

Most CEOs of companies have different mentors and advisers to help them understand parts of their business much faster than they could on their own. Other than books, Elon Musk also uses mentors as one of his main drivers for learning new things. Jim Cantrell served as Elon Musk's first mentor in rocket science. He was able to share his many years of rocket engineering experience with Elon, which greatly sped up Elon's learning curve. These mentors could be your boss at a company, a relative, or someone you reached out to. The way Elon Musk got Jim as his mentor was by cold calling him and explaining what he was trying to do with rockets. You could also see if the people you reached out to when figuring out what to learn as part of your MVK would be willing to serve as mentors during your learning journey.

5. Other students are another great resource for guidance and accountability. Having different student collaborations or study groups is the same as using them in the traditional model. Other students can sometimes help you understand things even better than mentors since they are just one step ahead of you, so they understand and relate to what you're going through better than a more seasoned mentor who is ten steps ahead. Connecting with other students could also be through live video, a phone call, or in person. Different industry forums are a great way to connect with other people learning the same thing and getting many of your questions answered. Some online courses also provide a way to connect with others taking the course.

Once you figure out which methods you prefer for learning, you can combine them to form your learning stack. This is simply your order and combination of learning methods. Most of the time people won't use every method available for learning as they prefer some methods over others. If someone is very poor at learning from books, then they might prioritize online courses as their go-to method for learning the fundamentals. The opposite could also be true. For short-form content some people by default might prefer videos vs. articles vs. podcasts. The same goes for having mentors or student study groups. People will also develop their own strategy over time for finding these resources and perfecting the way they learn from them.

As an example, someone's strategy could start by finding industry experts to serve as mentors and asking for recommendations on what books to read. Another person's strategy could be starting with searching Amazon for the top three books on the topic they want to learn. This is also part of my personal learning stack and strategy for learning a new topic. I've found there is currently more high-quality information in books than any other source, and I've developed my reading skills enough where I prefer books to online courses in most cases. As I read the books and find interesting sub-topics, I dig a little deeper into them by watching YouTube videos which also gives me a little break from reading. If I couldn't find enough on the topic through video, then I search for articles to read. By the time I'm done reading the books and articles, I'll have come across quite a few names of people who either wrote the books, wrote articles on the topic, or were referenced in the book or article. I'll then proceed to reach out to these people if I think a mentor could serve me well.

By first learning about the topic, it allows me to have deeper conversations with them and prove my interest in the topic, making it much more likely for them to help me. While this is my go-to strategy, I'll still use other resources if it makes sense for me on a case by case basis that often changes with different industries. For example, online forums are a very large part of the learning process for computer science, whereas, for sales, forums are a much smaller piece. Something else to note is that if there are certain industry certifications that employers place a high value on, then working towards getting them during this time could prove to be very valuable. For industries like information technology, certifications are a large part of the qualification process.

Where to Learn

While I was learning on my own, I was still able to get much of the college experience that people pay large amounts of money for. Most people don't realize you can still get the college experience without actually enrolling in college. No one is stopping you from hanging out on a public college campus or library. I've even shown up to a few different college classes that interested me, and I never had anyone tell me I couldn't be there. I even went as far as going to a few frat parties at GA Tech with some of the friends I made on campus. The only difference was that while everyone else was spending money on tuition, I was actually making money.

While you're utilizing this modern learning model, you could travel around the world or even live in student housing. You don't need to give up the college experience to go about learning this way. How much fun is the part where you sit inside a college classroom anyway? My sister, who was taking full-time online college classes moved near a campus of a different university to get the college experience like I was. She even met her husband there.

Not Enjoying It?

What happens if you aren't enjoying learning about the career? Do you just give up or do you push through? To answer this question, you need to identify why you aren't enjoying the learning process. There are two main categories this falls into.

1. Hypothesis misalignment. You went into this with a simple hypothesis that this career will be a great fit based on your goals, skills, and interests with the limited research you did. As you learn more about this career, you might find that the career doesn't align with your goals, skills, or interests like you originally thought. Perhaps it doesn't align with your goals since its career track is different than you envisioned or requires you to work somewhere you don't want to. This could cause you to lose motivation since you don't see this career helping you attain your goals. It's very important in this case to dig deep and understand if there is a way you might be able to reach your goals with this career. If you can't find a way, then your hypothesis about this career being a great fit was disproved based on it not aligning with your goals.

Perhaps you learn that the type of job you would be doing is different than you thought and requires a set of soft skills that aren't aligned with yours. This makes it very difficult for you to learn the material. Again, a good example of this would be a person thinking a marketing job would be a good fit since they have good communication skills but learns that it actually requires a much more technical and analytical skillset which is something this person isn't good at nor is interested in becoming good at. This newfound knowledge about the career also would disprove their hypothesis of it being a good fit based on the alignment with their skillset.

The last part of your hypothesis is that the career interests you. If this career meets your goals and skills, then it should interest you enough for you to want to make a career out of it. At the start of the learning process, the actual material you learn might not be of much interest. This is completely fine as we learned that interests take time to build. While it's preferable to start with at least some interest in what you're learning, it isn't unheard of to build an interest from scratch. Think about how interested you were in the material when you started learning about it and compare it to how interested you are in it after spending some time learning about it. Do you think you're more interested in it now than you were before? If so, then that's a very good sign. If your interest in the material is the only thing that lacks, then I'd give it more time to see if it grows on you before considering changing careers.

If you learn that either your goals or skills disprove your hypothesis, then it would be acceptable to go back to the bullseye and identify a new career to put through the learn/test cycle. It is very important to understand exactly why it is that this career wasn't a great fit so you can make sure you don't repeat your mistake. Also, you might have learned more about yourself during this time and could have slightly different goals or have different skills than you thought. You might have even discovered a new interest during this time that might be worth looking into to see if it fits in your bullseye.

2. Learning difficulty. This career could be very difficult to learn and require you to understand complex topics. This difficulty and confusion about the material could very well make you not enjoy the learning process. It's very important not to give up here as this difficulty can actually be looked upon as a good thing.

First, if the material is difficult for you, then it challenges you to be better and takes you out of your comfort zone. This difficulty is also the first of many in your career, so it's best to get used to it early. Overcoming learning difficult concepts is what levels you up and makes you smarter. You need to learn to enjoy breaking through these learning barriers. A book I highly recommend on getting through this difficulty is *The Obstacle Is the Way* by Ryan Holiday.

Secondly, this difficulty could be due to your lack of learning skills. You might lack the self-discipline required to learn on your own. This is great as it gives you an opportunity to improve your learning process and build your self-education skills, which will serve you throughout your life. During this time, you will need to find enjoyment in learning new things. This is also a great time to improve your reading skills to the point where you look forward to reading.

When I was in school, I absolutely hated reading and thought it wasn't for me until I began reading about things that interested me and would help accomplish my goals. I call this reading with purpose. I think a lot of other students are just like me where they were forced to read about subjects they weren't interested in during school, which made them associate reading with being boring and ultimately hating it. If this is you, it's imperative to self-correct this by reading about things out of choice that brings you closer to your goals. This time is also ideal to figure out your best learning strategy, the resources you learn best from, and in what combination.

7

Test

The third step, once you've learned the MVK of a career, is to test it. While all these principles will withstand time, the strategies which currently work in 2019 will likely change over time as perceptions around education are altered. This step is centered around the fundamental concept of rapid testing. In this rapid testing phase, you will either validate or invalidate your hypothesis of this being a great career that you want to expand on. You will know precisely how your perception of the career compares to the reality of it. This step will also provide you with relevant experience that companies put a high value on when making entry-level hiring decisions. This is your gateway into a full-time career. Everything you've been working towards so far leads you to get to this testing step as quickly as possible. You will learn at a much faster pace during this step as you finally have a chance to apply what you have learned while having direct guidance from great mentors within a company.

Internship vs. Apprenticeship vs. Entry-level Position

How do you know what type of role you should you use to run your test? There are three main types of roles to do this with the first being an internship. An internship is a trainee that works in a position with low or no pay in order to get the necessary work experience to qualify for a permanent position. Internships have a set duration normally lasting around three months. These internships are traditionally for college students during their summer break. The second type of role is apprenticeship. An apprenticeship is a system for training new practitioners of a trade or profession by working alongside an employer. This type of role is very common in the trades where people work with their hands and can lead to gaining a license to practice a regulated profession. The last type of role is an entry-level position. This is a permanent job requiring minimal and sometimes no experience. For companies with internship programs, entry-level positions that require some minimal experience are often filled by previous interns.

By doing your research and learning about the career, you should have some idea which route people typically use to break into that career. Each career is different with many of the more advanced entry-level white-collar careers requiring relevant or internship experience. The more simple or basic the career, the more likely they are to hire people directly into permanent positions. For careers in the trades, you will find apprenticeships to be the most common way of breaking in. You will need to figure out what the most common route is in the career you've chosen. A simple way to do this is by searching for other people on LinkedIn who have recently started their career in the same role and see what path they used. After looking at dozens of profiles, you should have a good idea of the most common ways to enter that career path.

If it turns out to be a career where there are multiple paths to breaking in, whether that's an entry-level position or internship, then it's important to choose the one where you will learn the most and be given the most responsibilities. During these early stages when you're searching for a position, you should always optimize for learning. The more you learn about yourself, the career, and improve your skills, the more likely you are to start a successful career. Your goal is not to make money during this test phase or have a strategic career plan. Your only goal of this testing cycle is to learn. After you've chosen a career that you want to expand on, then you can focus on making money and advancing your career.

What Companies Want

I'm sure you've heard people say that you need a college degree to get hired and they are partly right. From my experience, most companies do prefer candidates to have degrees, especially for white-collar business type jobs. There are, however, very few companies that will outright deny someone from working there if they don't have a degree. The challenge is getting your foot in the door without one. It's essential to understand why companies want candidates with a degree and where there is room for opportunity around "prefer." Before we dig into the reasons companies require degrees, lets first establish who is involved in the hiring process.

The first set of people involved in the hiring process is human resources. This group oversees a multitude of things such as payroll, benefits, handling disputes between employees, the culture, and recruiting new employees. Those working in human resources that are specifically tasked with hiring new employees are called recruiters. Their job involves a hiring manager asking them to find someone with a specific set of qualifications to do a job. These recruiters post all the job ads and do the initial interviewing to see if someone meets the basic qualifications set by the hiring manager. Their goal is only to pass along people they feel are qualified to the hiring manager who will interview them more in-depth. The recruiter has very little to do with the actual hiring decision once they pass the candidate to the hiring manager. Only sometimes will a person from HR be involved in the decision to make sure the candidate is a culture fit.

The second set of people involved in the hiring process are the hiring managers. A hiring manager is usually the head of a group or department within the company. When their team grows, or they have a need to hire someone new, then they will ask their recruiter to find someone with certain qualifications to fill that job. After the recruiter sends the hiring manager a candidate, they will interview them asking much more specific job-related questions and sometimes giving tests to prove they are qualified. If everything checks out and the hiring manager thinks they would make a good addition to their team, then they are normally able to proceed with a job offer. There is a chance that the manager would have to ask his boss for final approval to hire someone who doesn't have a degree. This is how most companies do their hiring with the smaller ones sometimes not having recruiters, which in that case, the hiring manager does the whole process.

Now, I'll identify three main reasons companies prefer candidates with degrees for entry-level jobs that people without degrees have to get around. The first reason is that there are simply too many applicants to choose from. With the current hiring process of posting jobs online and people applying in just minutes, there has been a huge influx of applicants. Within the first day of posting, there could be hundreds of applicants, and I've personally experienced this when I was hiring someone for a sales position. Most of the people that apply are not even remotely qualified, and if they are, they do an awful job of showing it. The number of applicants is overwhelming for recruiters at the companies so they need a way to filter down to the best ones since they couldn't possibly interview all of them. They usually only have a limited amount of information to filter down with such as a resume with their work experience and education and sometimes a cover letter. With internships or entry-level positions, they might not even have any work experience.

The government also has stringent recruiting regulations that put companies in a bad position of getting sued for discrimination. Recruiters must filter out people without risking someone claiming discrimination. One of the only completely legal ways to filter out people is based on formal education. After all, the general assumption is that people who went to college are probably going to be smarter, more motivated, and overall more qualified than the people who didn't. Many companies use online application programs that will automatically filter out people who don't have college degrees, so a recruiter will never even come in contact with the application.

The second reason is that most smart and motivated people who are capable of doing the job actually do go to college because they have been conditioned to do so by society. This means that even if a company is completely fine with hiring someone without a degree, they are likely going to end up hiring someone who has a degree because that's where the biggest pool of talent currently is. This puts companies in a difficult position because they don't want to lower the value and exclusivity of their job by saying it doesn't require a degree. This would make the people who have degrees not want the position since they want a job that would benefit them from having a degree. Taking a job without a degree requirement would make them feel like their degree is a waste and place them in the category of underemployed. The effect that this has on companies is them saying a degree is required or preferred on a job posting even if it isn't. This is their solution to attracting college graduates with the off chance of someone applying that is qualified but doesn't have a degree. I've recently spoken with a recruiter at a company whose job posting was very clear with a hard "degree required" stamped on it. The same recruiter that posted the ad told me that they don't really care if someone has a degree and actually just hired someone without a degree for that same position.

The last reason is that the hiring manager doesn't want to look bad. Once you get in front of the hiring manager and they can tell you're qualified to do the position and like you, then most won't really care if you have a degree or not. What they do care about is the chance that you don't work out, then they get questioned by their boss why they hired someone without a degree. This would make them look bad, so they prefer just to hire people with degrees, so they don't have to worry about this. In some cases, if they hired someone without a degree, then they would be the first hiring manager in the company to do so. This puts the spotlight on them and could backfire. The only way to get around this is by lowering the risk for the hiring manager. They need to have a very good reason why you're so much better than the other candidates with college degrees. They need to feel confident that you will work out. All your relevant education, experience, references, and the way you come across is going to impact this. Something that does help reduce this risk for the hiring manager are internships. Hiring someone in an internship is a fixed duration with minimal risk for the company. They don't expect everyone to be great or turn into permanent hires, so if someone doesn't work out it's not such a big deal.

Type of Company

Once you're clear on the path you're going to take to run your test, then the next step is to figure out what type of companies you want to target that hire people in your occupation. The main factors that come into play here are the size of the company and their industry.

The size of the company will have a big impact on your ability to break in, the structure you are given, and the diversity of your tasks. On one extreme it could be a one-person company, or on the other extreme, it could be a 100,000-person company. When choosing the size of a company, you should think more about your goals. If you want to be a writer, then do you want to write articles for a large company and move up the corporate chain, or do you want to be an accomplished author? If your goal is to write articles for a large company, then starting at a large company would probably help you get closer to that goal while maximizing your learning on what it takes to write articles for a large company. If your goal is to be an author, then working directly with an author would probably help you get closer to that while maximizing your learning on what it takes to be an author. Ultimately, your goal should be to work with the people you aspire to be like. The difficulty of breaking into large versus small companies is also very apparent. The very well known, large companies often attract the smartest people from the top schools, making it very competitive to get into these types of companies.

The smaller or lesser-known companies don't get that same attention, so breaking in is often significantly easier. A lot of people start their careers at smaller companies to get their foot in the door and then later transition to a larger company. This is especially true for people without college degrees since small companies don't have the same policies or politics that larger companies do. If you do choose to start at a smaller company, then they often won't have the same structure for training in place that large companies do. This can make it difficult for someone who relies on others for direction instead of taking the initiative. The more comfortable you are with ambiguity, then the more you will like smaller companies due to the greater amount of autonomy you have to make decisions and control your work.

The industry the company works in could also be important to you. For example, if you are like me and specialized in sales development, then there are a few different industries that often hire for that role. You could work in a company that sells software, hardware, or services. This could be important because if you already have a particular interest in an industry, then you could use it in your favor for further separating yourself from the others. What you learn during the test could also differ slightly based on the industry the company is in. You can also work back from your goals here to see if one industry would get you closer to reaching them than another one would.

Positioning

The way you present and position yourself is vitally important if you don't have a college degree. Unfortunately, in our current society, people will want to bucket you in the category of uneducated people who aren't smart enough to go to college. You must change their perception of you from uneducated to self-educated. This positioning starts before you ever even talk to a person. They will judge you based on your resume, and once they have your name, they can google you and find your LinkedIn profile or other social media posts. Everything they see will either confirm their current perception of you being uneducated or build their perception of you being self-educated.

Think about all the time and money you saved by not going to college. Part of all this time you saved should be spent improving how you position yourself. Employers will be looking for reasons not to hire you, so you need to completely change their outlook. Your ability to appropriately position yourself will also serve you throughout your entire life. You must be better than everyone else you're competing with in all the following departments.

1. Resume. The first thing you must perfect is your resume. It should be immaculate and tailored to the occupation you want to test, along with the type of company you want to work for. When a hiring manager sees your resume, they should immediately think you're a perfect fit. It should include a section about why you want to work specifically in this particular role and for the company you're applying to. Under experience, you should include all relevant work experience, accomplishments, and what you learned from it that would help you do this job. Even if you don't think your previous experience or accomplishments are relevant, you should still be able to think of a way to tie in how they helped improve some of the skills that are critical to being successful in your occupation. Under education, you should include all the specific skills and knowledge you learned for this job. You should also include some of the resources you used or ways you went about learning and improving these skills. "I prepared myself to get this job by improving these skills and learning

_____ things through _____ and I learned how to effectively_____." The person looking at your resume will want to see indications that you're qualified to do this role and have a strong interest in it. Everything about your resume should lead them to that conclusion.

2. LinkedIn. LinkedIn has become one of the greatest tools for making yourself look professional. It is the modern version of the resume that is almost always one of the first things hiring managers will search for. You will need to make sure both your LinkedIn profile and resume are kept up to date with each other. Some pro tips for LinkedIn would be to spend some money and get a professional headshot of you taken. This alone will do quite a bit for showing companies you care and helping remove you from that category of uneducated. Not many college students take the time to do this, so it is a very good initial differentiator. Some other things to work on regarding your LinkedIn would be to get 500 plus connections who are insiders in the field. This will make you very likely to show up as having common connections to the hiring managers at the companies you want to work at. This is a great indication to employers that you have a strong interest in the career. Your LinkedIn profile can never be too good, so you should constantly be focused on improving it.

3. Google and social media presence. Employers will often search your name in Google to see what comes up. This can either make you or break you. When employers search entry-level candidates, they expect to find nothing related to the career and hopefully nothing that would deter them from wanting to hire you. Not only must you eliminate anything that would deter them, but you should also create content they could find that would make them perceive you as being self-educated and knowledgeable about the occupation. One of the things you can do to position yourself well on Google is to have your own website, preferably your name, displaying a portfolio of accomplishments and education. You can actually create your own resources profile on CourseCareers.com which will display all the resources you used to learn from. This profile will also show up at the top of Google when someone searches for your name. You can also create content around the career you're learning about by writing blog posts, creating YouTube videos, and posting on forums. These are all great ways to show your knowledge about a career while improving your Google presence.

How to Get Hired

You learned if you apply online, your application will likely just go into a pile without ever being seen. If you were somehow able to get past this automated filter, then at the very best you will have your resume seen by a recruiter who also has 50 other people to choose from who do have college degrees. With the recruiter having no real understanding of the position when deciding on who to interview, they will likely stick with what they know and interview someone that has a relevant degree. After all, they don't want to look bad in front of the hiring manager by sending them someone who doesn't even have a degree, making them look like they can't do their job. This is why you should try to skip the recruiter all together and go straight to the hiring manager. This is the three-step process for how you do that.

1. List Building. The first step in this process is to put together a list of companies you want to target. These will be companies that are aligned with the criteria you've set based on their size and industry. These companies must also be hiring for the entry point you've decided to test your occupation through. One of the best ways I've found to put together this list is by simply searching jobs boards for the position you're looking for. You can then run a quick Google or LinkedIn search on the company to see if it fits within your criteria. If it looks like a good fit, then add that company name and job posting link to the list. I recommend you try to identify 10-20 companies to start with.

After you've compiled this list of companies, you will need to figure out who the hiring manager is at each of these companies for the position you want. One way you can do this is by going to the company's LinkedIn profile and searching for all their employees. You can then filter down based on the position you're interested in and find the associated director or manager in charge of hiring for the position. You will need to repeat this until you have found all the people you suspect of being the hiring manager at these companies and added them to your list. Something to take note of though is that the correct hiring manager is very often in the same location as the role they are hiring for. If you're not completely sure if they're the right person, go ahead and add them to the list anyway.

The last missing piece of our list is the contact information of these hiring managers. For the most part, this contact information will just consist of their email and the companies corporate phone number. The best way to get their email address without spending thousands on buying data is to use an educated guess. I found that in over 90% of the cases, I'm able to find someone's company email address this way. For this to work, you will need to use a website that can test if an email is valid or not. I personally found that NeverBounce is one of the best free services for this, but there are a number of websites that provide this service for free. You will then want to try every regular combination of their name @ the company's domain name. Some names might be a short version of their real name, so if you can't find it, then you could try the extended version of their name. Some examples of this for John Doe that works at XYZ company would be:

john.doe@xyz.com

john@xyz.com

doe@xyz.com

johndoe@xyz.com

john.d@xyz.com

john_doe@xyz.com

john_d@xyz.com

jdoe@xyz.com

johnd@xyz.com

Run through all of these until you have a valid email for each of the hiring managers in your list. If you still can't find it, then you can also search for a different person at the same company and see if you can validate theirs. Once you have one person's email at the company, then it is almost always the same for the other employees. To find the company's corporate phone number, you should be able to just google "*company name* corporate phone number." You should also be able to find it on their website. Add both the email addresses and phone numbers to your list.

2. Outreach. This is the second step in the process and the most time-consuming. You will need to actively put yourself out there and get in front of the hiring managers. This means doing anything necessary to get their attention.

- Even though your application is very unlikely to make it through the online screening process, go ahead and spend the time applying to each of the companies on your list. Be sure to include a great cover letter if possible. This cover letter should be tailored to the company showing you did your homework on them. The reason you're applying first is just so it will give you something to reference when you reach out to the hiring manager.
- Do some initial research on each company and the associated contact to be able to mention something relevant about what they're looking for or the industry they are in. You should know the high-level history of each company and contact. You should know their products, services, or technologies and what type of people buy their products or services. By doing your homework, it shows the hiring manager for each company that you actually invested your time and care about working there. You can do this research by reading about each company on their website while also reading articles about them. To research the hiring manager contacts, you can look at their LinkedIn profiles and read any articles or posts they wrote. This research is one of the many things that helps you position yourself as a professional self-educated person while setting you apart since most other applicants don't take the time to do this research.
- Once you've done your initial research on each company, then you will need to reach out to each hiring manager simultaneously. This outreach should be treated as a sales process with your goal being to get an interview with one or

more of the hiring managers. This means you need to understand there will be rejection and that's just part of the process. Just like a sales process, you will have multiple ways to connect with the hiring managers. You can use the phone, email, social media, or in person. Your outreach strategy should consist of using a combination of these ways to get in touch with the managers. Here is an example of a set of actions you can follow for reaching out to each hiring manager.

Day 1: 1st Email

Day 2: 1st Phone call

Day 4: Send a LinkedIn message

Day 5: 2nd Phone call

Day 6: 2nd Email

Day 6: Like or comment on their LinkedIn post

Day 8: 3rd Phone call in the morning

Day 8: 4th Phone call in the evening

Day 9: Stop and add different companies

While this might seem like a lot, it's important to realize that these hiring managers are busy people and they could easily overlook your message, so it's important to try multiple times through every source to give yourself the best chance of getting noticed. After all, they need you just as much if not more than you need them. You should use a spreadsheet to keep track of what actions you have done for each company. This will keep you organized and stay consistent. As far as what you should say in these messages, they should only consist of a few sentences with the focus being why you're interested in the position along with asking for a time to talk.

Some of the people that might have served as mentors in the industry to you during this time could act as a great resource. You should tell these people what type of position you are looking for and ask if they can introduce you to anyone they know. If you're able to get referred by someone in the industry, that will go a long way to getting you hired.

Another way you can get in contact with hiring managers is by connecting with them in person. Meeting these people in person is always better if possible. If you're able to make a good impression in person, then the chance of you getting an interview that will turn into a job offer is much higher. The first way you can meet these hiring managers is by showing up to the same organizations or events they attend. You can normally find these organizations by looking at the LinkedIn profile for each of the hiring managers on your list and seeing which organizations they belong to. You can also figure out which industry events are going on by running an internet search for " _____ events in my city."

By attending college career fairs, it is sometimes possible to meet these hiring managers. Employers that attend these career fairs are looking to hire interns or entry-level people, so they are perfect. To find career fairs near you, you will need to search for all the events at local colleges. If you find a career fair that is relevant to your field, then add it to your calendar. Whenever you show up to one of these events, you will want to dress professionally with resumes in hand just like the other students. You might need to do a little bit of finessing to get in. Once you get in, you should talk to every company and ask them intelligent industry-specific questions that show you know what you're talking about. If you have a list of companies that will be attending, you should do your homework on the ones you're interested in beforehand. If they ask what your major is, then don't be afraid to tell them that you're self-educated and just here to meet employers. Chances are it won't be as big of a deal as you think with some employers being impressed by it.

Your goal of these in-person meetings is to learn the basics about what they're looking for to make sure it's a good fit while also proving to them your interest and ability to do the job. After talking with them for a few minutes, you should be able to ask for a time on their calendar to have a more in-depth discussion. This could be over the phone or in-person with the latter being the most preferable.

3. Interview. The interview is the last step in the process once you've set up a time to talk with the hiring manager. It's important to remember that this first interview is no more than a conversation to see if both you and the employer are a good fit for each other. Keep in mind that they need good people just as much as you need a good job.

Here is what a typical hiring process looks like:

Step 1: Screen. This is normally done by human resources or the recruiter to see if you match the qualifications they were told to look for by the hiring manager. Hopefully, you were able to talk directly to the hiring manager and skip this step.

Step 2: Phone Interview. This will probably be with the hiring manager and is the first conversation to see if you would both be a good fit for each other. You will likely start the process here.

Step 3: In-Person Interview. This interview will normally be more in-depth and could involve multiple decision-makers, such as the hiring manager's boss or HR to see if you are a culture fit.

Step 4: Offer Made. This is when they have decided they want to hire you and extend a formal offer.

The one word that can describe if an interview will go well or not is preparation. Everything you've done so far is preparing for this interview. Everything you've learned about the career will be shown during the interview. The positioning you've done to set yourself apart from others will be looked at positively by the hiring manager. After you've set up a time to interview with the company, there are several things you should do to prepare. It's important to do much more in-depth research after you've scheduled an interview. You need to understand exactly what the position entails and everything about the company. You should know the company history, major recent events, their competition, main value to the market, etc.

I was reading an article about how a woman got an interview with Google and read an entire book just on the company history before she went in for the interview. She said that her knowledge of their history impressed the recruiter so much that it eventually led to her getting the job. You do not want to skip out on doing everything you can to learn about the company. By doing in-depth research and preparation, you really stand out compared to nearly every other entry-level candidate.

You should anticipate every question that they will ask you during the interview and have responses to them. These questions could range from general interview questions to industry-specific questions that will require you to use some of the knowledge you have learned. You need to do better in this interview than everyone else so the company will have no reason not to hire you other than you just not having a degree. With all the time you invested in the previous steps, you do not want to screw up by not investing enough time preparing for the interview.

Lastly, you will need to dress appropriately for the interview. This normally means dressing one step above what employees normally wear at the company, and typically this would be either business casual or business professional. You will also want to have a copy of your resume along with a list of references with contact information. I suggest you give yourself plenty of time to get to the interview location to make sure there is absolutely no chance you're late, however, only walk into the building about five minutes before your meeting.

During the interview, you will need to focus on presenting yourself as the self-educated professional you've been positioning yourself as. This means when they ask about your education, you can describe to them that you're self-taught and proceed to list some of the resources you used to prepare for the position. You must first believe in yourself if you want the company to believe in you. You should also teach the hiring manager about your unique value coming from a self-educated background. For example, one of your strengths you can mention is your ability to learn very quickly on your own. You are also an ambitious self-starter who is skilled at working with minimal direction. Remember that companies put a high value on these things, so you should take pride in your self-education background.

If the position is an internship, then you can pitch them on the benefits of hiring a self-educated intern instead of a traditional college intern. Unlike a college intern, you can work as an intern full-time anytime of the year and can be transitioned into a full-time employee immediately without having to wait to graduate. If you can communicate these benefits to the company, it could open their mind up about hiring you as an intern. This is especially true if the company is known for only hiring college interns during the summer.

After the interview is over, you can follow up with a handwritten letter or email thanking them for taking the time to interview you and letting them know you're looking forward to their decision. You should also note down which questions they asked you that you did a poor job of answering so you can improve for your next interview. While you're waiting for their decision, you should still be reaching out to other companies and trying to get interviews with them. By going through the interview process with multiple companies, it gives you a backup if the company you want most decides not to hire you. You can also use other offers as leverage to get hired faster or for a higher salary.

During the Test

What should you do during the test to make sure it's a success? The goal of the test is to learn if this is a career you want to expand on, and if it is, it can act as a gateway to a full-time position. This means you will need to learn as much as you possibly can about the position during this time to make an informed decision on whether this is the right career for you. You will also need to do a very good job, so if you do decide you want to start your career here, then you will likely be promoted to a permanent employee. With most internships lasting 3-4 months, you will need to give 150% during this time. You should show up early and leave late. You should take direction from your boss and do great work at even the seemingly meaningless tasks you might be given. This is your time to shine.

With your first goal being to learn, everything you do should be optimized for learning as much as you can about the career. When you focus everything on learning as much as possible, it will not only help you make a better decision on your career choice but also show your managers how driven you are. Everything you do is a chance for you to apply what you have learned while taking advantage of on the job training. With application and guidance from someone in the company, you will learn at a much faster rate than on your own. This is why it's so important to make the most of this opportunity while you have it.

It could benefit you to talk to entry-level employees that are in the same position that you want and figure out what skills you lack to be able to do the job effectively. You can ask them for advice on what to learn or focus your efforts on. You can learn from them what it's like to work at the company and what it takes to succeed there. Don't be afraid to ask for this guidance as these people can also act as internal supporters that can sway the decision on who the manager hires for a permanent position. The more of these internal supporters you build during this time, the better. You should also try to build an internal supporter from the person who matters most, your manager. To build this supporter, you should focus on doing great work at the tasks you are assigned and finishing before they are due by working harder and smarter. You can then use your extra time to ask the manager if there is anything you can do to take work off their plate. If they give tasks to you, then that's just more opportunity to learn. If they don't, then it's still a great gesture that shows you're willing to do more than asked and will carry you a long way when they consider who to promote. Something to also note down is that if you ask for advice, you better be listening well enough to follow through on it and any other commitments you make.

Once you're in the role and doing the job, you're finally on an even playing field with the others who went to college. You are only being judged on the quality of work you do. It's very easy to use your specialized knowledge and self-education skills here to do better quality work than other people if you put your mind to it. The only reason for you to not get hired afterward is because they don't have any available positions open. Even in that case, they should have been so impressed by your work that they will go out of their way to refer you to other employers they know in the industry if you ask.

Criteria for Success or Failure

If you're still unclear about whether you should stick with the career or change careers after your test, then you should start with the basics of what makes a great career and how your expectations compared to the reality.

First, look at your career goals. Do you think this career will meet your career goals like you thought it would or did you learn more about yourself during this time, and your career goals have actually changed? If your career goals have changed, do your new goals align with this career?

Next, look at the required skills. Did this career use the same skills you thought it would? Did you learn that you weren't as skilled in this like you thought you were? If you struggled during this time, do you think it was because your boss didn't give you clear instructions or guidance? Do you think the expectations set for you were unrealistic? Would a different boss make it easier? Did you improve your skills during this time? Are you proud of the improvements you made?

Last, does this career still pique your interest? Did the day to day duties of the career entail what you thought it would? Was this type of work for interns or permanent employees? What type of work do more senior people do and how long does it take to get there? Are you interested in that work or where the career might lead you? Did you find your interest in the career grow or diminish during the test?

Hopefully answering these questions helped clear up some things and align the most important things you want out of life. With this being a very important decision, it's advisable to really spend time thinking through the pros and cons of both sticking with the career and switching careers. Ask yourself if you don't do this, then what would you do? Is it worth the resources, effort, and risk trying to test a different career?

There are a couple of things to keep in mind. You don't need to have everything planned out. Your goal might only be to get an entry-level job that pays enough money to live on your own. After you accomplish that goal, you may think of a bigger or completely different career goal you want to go after. Perhaps you will find this meets all your career goals and you derive happiness from other more personal goals. A famous quote from Mike Tyson is "everyone has a plan until they get punched in the face." Many people's plans never come to fruition, so just take one step at a time while you're continuously searching and figuring out what your next step in life will be.

The second thing to keep in mind is that an entry-level position is like the trunk of a fruit tree. It branches out in a seemingly endless number of ways with all the rewards being at the end of the branches. It takes time to get to the fruit. You must be willing to climb up from the bottom to get there.

The Cycle

If you do decide you want to run another testing cycle with a different career, then you should know that the next one will be easier. During your first test, you learned more about what you want and what you are good at. These new findings will help you identify a better career fit, making your next test much more likely to be a success.

You also discovered how to learn in this modern economy and acquired many hard and soft skills which can be transferred to a new career you test. This will significantly speed up the pace at which you reach the MVK of the new career you choose. You've already gone through the major grunt work for positioning yourself to be ready for a company to hire you, so all you have to do is change a few things to align with the new career you test. With just a few cycles of testing, it is almost guaranteed you will find a great career for yourself

8

Expand

You've just had a successful test and have done great in your first role, enough so that you got promoted to a permanent position, or perhaps, you were one of the lucky ones who was able to start in a permanent position. Either way, you are now tasked with doing well in this new position to either maintain it or get promoted based on what your goals are at this time.

Now What?

No matter what your career goals are, you will need to be expanding your education. You didn't try to predict and cram a lifetime worth of knowledge into four years. Instead, you specialized so you can have a better and more efficient way of acquiring the knowledge you will need in your career along the way. The best way to expand is by using the fundamental concept of just in time education. This concept serves as your education strategy for reaching your goals. As you learned before, this just in time concept is for reducing waste that would occur if you learn something only to never use it and have it erode away over time. This belief also entails using the internet to store information that is easier to access through research rather than through memory.

To reduce educational waste while improving the effectiveness of the education to reach your career goals, you should only focus on learning what's necessary for you to reach the next logical step in your goal. This means that if your goal is to become a manager, then you need to figure out what is required to reach that manager position. If you learn that to become the manager you must first meet certain goals or be exceptional in your current job, then the next logical step for your education is to focus on learning things that will make you reach those goals and be exceptional in the role you're in right now. Once you learn enough to become exceptional, then you can figure out what else you need to learn to progress to the following step as manager. It's important to remember that you never really know what the next set of things you will have to learn is until you get to that point. This is why it's important to break down your goal into attainable steps, so you only focus on learning what is required to accomplish one step at a time.

You then repeat the process of figuring out what you must learn to reach the next step of your goal. One of the great benefits of breaking down your goals into steps and focusing on the learning required for one step at a time is that you're much more likely to actually reach your career goals. This is because you know you are moving in the right direction and making progress every time you reach a new step instead of trying to learn everything at once and feeling lost. It allows you to focus your efforts on learning the most valuable things that will have the most significant direct impact on your career. This is how many successful people that became great entrepreneurs or executives approached their education.

As an example of breaking goals into attainable steps, my goal of writing this book was actually split up into many different steps. This was because writing a book was a massive goal for me since I had never written one before. For me, trying to learn how to write a book all at once would be like trying to eat a whole elephant. At the start, it seems impossible until you split it up into one bite at a time just like writing a book seemed impossible to me until I split it up into many attainable steps. The first step was to figure out what I was going to write by creating a mind map, so then I had to learn how to create a mind map. After I accomplished that step, I figured out my next step was to compile my mind map into an outline. Once I learned how to create my outline, I needed to figure out how to write my first rough draft. Once I accomplished my goal of writing the draft, I went onto the next step of editing. After I'm finished editing, I will need to figure out how to format and publish the book. For each one of these steps, I didn't know how to accomplish the following step until I finished the one at hand. This is what allowed me to stay focused on making progress without getting overwhelmed. Without breaking this goal into steps, I don't think I would have been able to finish.

Now that you understand the just in time strategy for continued learning, you should understand the many options available for continuing your education. While these options will use many of the same resources you used to learn the MVK for your career choice, there are also quite a few businesses, such as Lynda and Skillshare, being built with the purpose of furthering the education of professionals. In our modern world, there is no longer a need to rely on college to expand your knowledge. For example, if the next step in your goal of becoming a manager involves becoming a great speaker, then you can take classes in speaking. There are many classes to choose from including in-person classes on traditional college campuses or through companies such as General Assembly. You also have an endless number of online courses you can take in speaking. Your job is to figure out which works best for you for what you're trying to learn or improve. In a situation where it's speaking, an in-person setting will have advantages that an online course cannot replicate. The vast majority of online courses are actually built for continued professional education instead of starting careers. Many companies will even have subscriptions to these course websites giving their employees unlimited access. You will probably find that it is much easier to expand your career education compared to starting it.

The other part of just in time education is using the internet and other resources as your warehouse for bits of information. The internet will almost always produce a more reliable answer than you can produce from your memory of information you might have learned years ago. This ability to consistently be able to pull reliable information from the internet whenever you need it is a skill that you need to work on improving. Think about all the time that could be wasted trying to memorize different facts that could be attained in a simple google search or a five-minute YouTube video. You should work on putting part of this time you saved into learning how to do expert research. This means being able to find any information you want in a very quick and repeatable manner. Just like your learning strategy, you should also have an information strategy. You should figure out which resources you prefer to pull information from and get very good at using those resources. This will serve as one of your greatest assets and make you feel like an information superhero.

Making Moves

Something so many people worry about for no reason is getting stuck. They think that without a college degree they won't be able to make any career progress and be stuck in the same entry-level job for the rest of their life. This is flat out false. There are an endless number of changes you can make in your career. These changes are categorized into either horizontal moves or vertical moves. Horizontal moves are when you move to a similar position without much, if any, gain in pay or responsibility. This isn't a promotion, but rather just a different job at the same level you were currently at. Vertical moves, known as climbing the corporate ladder, are when you move to a more advanced position with more pay and responsibility. This type of move is a promotion. You can make an endless number of both horizontal and vertical moves based on your goals and motivation to reach them.

An example of a successful horizontal move would be someone specializing in a sales role and starting at a company in an entry-level position. While this person might be able to perform the role successfully, they don't have ambitions to become the best salesperson or move up the sales chain as a manager. This person would rather work in human resources, so they get transferred to work as an entry-level recruiter. While this person didn't get a promotion or increase their pay, they did, however, get to work in a different job that they enjoy more and might want to make vertical moves with.

An example of a successful vertical move would be another person working in the entry-level sales position and doing such a great job they get promoted to a senior sales rep with additional responsibilities and pay.

While you're debating what type of moves you should make, it's important to strive to reach mastery. This is the point where you know something so well in your field that you are seen as an expert by others. This is where you will be able to get the fruit of the tree. This is the fruit of hard work and persistence that you put in to reach mastery, something that few people reach, thus making you very high in demand. The people that become executives or build companies reached mastery in their field. It takes time to get to that point, and typically most people running a company are at least in their forties. This mastery involves constantly getting better at what you do every day, learning step by step how to reach your next vertical goal.

Someone who comes to mind when I think of working from the bottom until reaching mastery is Andrew Carnegie, a man who became one of the richest people in the world. He got his start by working as a messenger in a telegraph office for $2.50 a week. He became very good at it and was known for being the best. This led to him being promoted vertically to a telegraph operator doubling his salary to $5 a week. He was able to continue working his way up until he was the personal assistant to Thomas Scott working for the Pennsylvania Railroad. Under Scott, Carnegie learned all about railroads and investing, which is what put Carnegie on the path to making his first million. From there, Carnegie was well on his way to building his empire.

While most people couldn't dream of how a $2.50 a week telegraph job would lead to riches, Carnegie was able to create an opportunity for himself in whichever role he worked by doing the best job he could and taking pride in it. I would be willing to bet that no matter where Carnegie started, he would always find a way for it to lead him to riches. With every new job you work or thing you learn, it opens opportunities to move both vertically and horizontally. Your new promotion then leads to more opportunities that weren't possible or even conceivable before through this never-ending cycle of endless opportunity. If you want to learn more about this, then I suggest you read the book *Mastery* by Robert Green.

Changing Companies

What if your goal is to make a vertical or horizontal move but you can't at your current company? What if you want a different boss? What if you want to move to a different city? Changing companies may not be as difficult as you think. When changing jobs your education is a much smaller piece of the decision than it was when you got your internship or first job. For your second job, they look at your experience and accomplishments much more than your education because your experience and accomplishments are a much better indicator for future success. This is why you will often see job postings for senior roles substituting the requirement for education with work experience. The status of the company in your occupation will also have a big impact on how other companies value you. For example, if you're a software engineer at Google, then other companies will put a premium on you as they think you must be great if Google hired you.

While strategically switching companies to advance your career is a very complicated subject that I'm sure many have written entire books on, I've compiled a list of a few important things you should do to prepare yourself to switch companies.

1. You need to do great work at your current company for at least one year. Anything less than one year could show up as a red flag to employers, causing them to think twice about investing their time in you, thinking you may leave soon. It's important to learn as much as you can at your current company and do an excellent job so you can easily transition to another company. While doing a great job, you will also want to be building references at the company from people such as your coworkers and managers that will back you up even when you switch companies. If you don't build these references, then how is a new company supposed to validate your claims? Since you only have a slim amount of work experience, it's absolutely necessary to build these supporters for you in your current company. These bosses or other employees you befriend could also move on to other companies where they will likely need to hire people in your position. If they were asked to refer someone to work there, you should be first on their mind. After all, internal references carry much more weight for getting hired than pretty much anything else you can do.

2. A great strategy for getting noticed by companies is by becoming a thought leader in your industry through content creation. Once you become very knowledgeable in your role and industry, then you should begin creating content to help teach others what you know. This could involve writing articles, making YouTube videos, or posting on social media. If this is your first job and you're working in the nitty-gritty of very basic tasks, then you might understand the minute details of the job that improve your work. These are things that people working at a higher level in your industry might not be aware of. If you're able to teach them something about their own industry, they will immediately classify you as an expert in the job who is the best at what you do. This makes you a scarce commodity and something that hiring managers will flock to get on their team. What makes this especially lucrative is that other entry-level people are very unlikely to be creating content, so it is easy to stand out. This thought leadership is often how people will land positions at top companies that otherwise only hire from a select pool of candidates. I've read many stories of people getting jobs at some of the best companies in the world using this strategy.

3. It is also very important to get job offers from other companies before leaving your current job. This is universally accepted between everyone in the workforce and one of your greatest tools for leverage. Some employers actually discount people that aren't currently employed thinking they must not be any good if someone hasn't already hired them. If you were to leave a company and only have a fixed amount of time before you run out of money, you are probably more open to accepting a less than optimal offer. If you're still working and have no urgency, you can easily turn down offers until you get one that satisfies you.

The Lifelong Learning Mindset

Learning is a lifelong process that is a never-ending journey. This is exactly the kind of mindset you will need to have every day as you should always be striving to learn new things. All successful people commit to this lifelong learning mindset. You need to learn to enjoy this learning process and constantly seek ways to improve it.

Once you've accomplished your goal of starting your career, you can spend more time on recreational learning. You've heard about people saying how college makes you a well-rounded individual and the importance of that. Perhaps you want to become more well-rounded. You've already learned how to learn so go learn about economics, politics, history, science, or anything you're interested in. Do you want to take on a project and renovate your house? Now that you know how to learn, go ahead and learn how to do that renovation. You're an education powerhouse. Anything you want to do is within your grasp. All you have to do is learn how to do it. You can take time to travel around the world and learn about other cultures or different languages. While this learning is for your own interests, you never know if it might benefit your career in unexpected ways. You could learn about a business or investment opportunity, perhaps even have a more intelligent conversation with a senior executive at your dream company.

The more you learn about things that interest you, the more you will enjoy the learning process. This education could end up leading you somewhere you never thought was possible. When I was working as a sales rep and had a goal of building a company, I spent nearly every lunch hour learning about how to be an entrepreneur. This type of education really interested me, so I spent hours every night reading up on different case studies of successful companies. I was able to put my learning skills to their fullest use by learning about building companies from the ground up and solving big problems. I also found it interesting to learn about economics and politics. For fun, I read books such as *The Autobiography of Benjamin Franklin* and *The Wealth of Nations*; books that most people couldn't imagine having to read even if they were required to in a college class. While I have a passion for sales, startups, and solving this college education problem, I've also found a passion for learning. I hope everyone reading this book will also find their passion for learning.

Conclusion

Congratulations. You're now part of a select group of people who understand how to start their career in a very efficient and effective manner without having to rely on college.

The Future

There are many very smart people who predict the downfall of our university system in the coming years. Will colleges collapse like the newspaper industry? What will this downfall look like, and what will the future of education entail? Clay Christensen is a Harvard professor and author of one of the best-known books on innovation, *The Innovator's Dilemma*. He also wrote a book titled *The Innovative University*. He's been studying and teaching how industries have entirely changed through technological innovation for years and even coined the term disruptive innovation which you will likely hear at some point in your career. Christensen has predicted that 50% of all universities will be bankrupt in the US within 10-15 years. In 2017 he even doubled down on that claim by lowering his estimate to maybe nine years.

Another prominent person with a deep understanding of higher education is Jeff Selingo. He has been writing about higher education for over 20 years and published three books on the subject with his most popular being *College Unbound*. Jeff talks about how while he doesn't think all universities will just disappear, he does believe they will be radically different places in ten years with a personalized online, hybrid education being a big part of that change.

Have you ever heard someone say that we are in a student loan bubble or a college bubble? There are many people that will throw these phrases around on the news, yet they never take the time to explain what this means and what kind of impact it will have. Let's start by defining what a bubble is. Investopedia's definition of a bubble is "an economic cycle characterized by the rapid escalation of asset prices followed by a contraction. It is created by a surge in asset prices unwarranted by the fundamentals of the asset and driven by exuberant market behavior. When no more investors are willing to buy at the elevated price, a massive selloff occurs, causing the bubble to deflate." In layman's terms, this means that if something is priced higher than it is worth, then the price will go down all at once.

So, what is college worth? In chapter two, you learned about the value of college being composed of three parts: the network, the education, and the experience. The value of the network of a college degree continues to decrease as more and more companies such as Google, IBM, and Apple speak publicly on how they no longer require degrees for many positions. There have also been many people talking about how students shouldn't go to college and all the abundant alternatives. Also, the amount of people working as hiring managers in companies without degrees has continued to rise. The value of the network comes from how many people think having a degree is important, and the level of importance they place on it. Since these two factors have continued to erode, the value of the network has also eroded with it.

The value of the education also continues to decrease at a very fast pace as online education becomes readily available to everyone at a fraction of the price. Why would you pay $100,000 to learn about economics from an average state school professor when you could learn it from some of the smartest people in the world for nearly free? The internet has allowed for full in-depth course material to always be up to date and accessed by anyone. Instead of one teacher giving a lecture to the 100 students they have in a class, they can instead give that lecture to a million people from around the world without having any of the infrastructure cost that comes with being in a classroom.

The last part of the value is the experience. This value has continued to rise over the years as colleges use the experience as their primary way to attract students. However, the problem with this is that the experience isn't what gets people jobs like 80% of freshmen enrolled in college want. This means that when people think they are buying insurance for their future or an investment to get a good job, they are actually just buying a consumption good in the form of the college experience. While this experience is worth something, most people wouldn't be willing to pay the inflated price if they realized it was only a consumption good.

So, what does this mean? Well, the value of college continues to decrease rapidly as the cost of college continues to increase rapidly. This causes the return on investment also to decrease rapidly, making the college degree much less valuable from a financial perspective. The current student loan default rate is 11% and increasing. Jeff Selingo noted that a survey, run in 2018 by the Chronicle of Higher Education, Council of Independent Colleges, and the American Association of State Colleges and Universities, found 55% of private colleges and 52% of public colleges fell short of their net-tuition revenue. The same survey found that 44% of public colleges and 52% of private colleges didn't meet their enrollment goals. With all these numbers increasing while being in one of the best economies in history, it's easy to see why people like Mark Cuban think we are in a bubble.

I predict that when the economy goes into another downturn, and many of the entry-level jobs are lost, then this student loan default rate will skyrocket. This is when people will realize that the asset value (price of college) is too high and unwarranted by the fundamentals of the asset (ability to get high paying jobs). This will pop the bubble as no more investors (students and parents) will be willing to buy at the elevated price. This will cause a massive sell-off to occur (people no longer enrolling in college). The bubble will then deflate (many colleges will go bankrupt and disappear or restructure).

The reason this affects you is because the value of having a college degree will significantly decrease after this bubble bursts, making the degree itself nearly worthless. This is due to the network of many colleges disappearing as they go bankrupt and the vast amount of companies that will stop requiring degrees. You don't want to owe huge amounts of money on a degree that isn't worth anything in a down economy where it's hard to get a good-paying job.

If you look back around 2008 when the economy tanked, the recent graduates also had a tough time. Many of the students that graduated in the recession had to move back home with their parents since they couldn't find a job to support themselves. Hiring projections according to the National Association of Colleges and Employers went down nearly 22% in Spring of 2009. The Education Department's National Center for Education Statistics said that Americans who received bachelor's degrees in 2008 were roughly twice as likely to be unemployed after a year than were their peers who graduated in 1993 and 2000. Some estimate that it can take as long as 15 years for students that graduated in the recession to catch up to students who graduated just a few years later. Imagine all of this but many times worse. That's what you can expect when the college bubble bursts

What happens to education after the bubble pops? Imagine seeing your friends with over $40,000 in debt struggle to get jobs in restaurants or fast food that pay minimum wage. After students see many of their peers significantly crippled by loads of debt with no job prospects, I predict the number one thing on their minds would be to get training that leads directly to a good career without going into debt. This will most likely lead students to look for different types of online education with four-year degrees being a thing of the past for many. The universities that do survive the initial wave from a substantial decrease in enrollment will have to significantly increase tuition for the students that remain to cover their high fixed costs. The value of college degrees will simultaneously decrease at an incredibly fast pace as companies will continue dropping degree requirements and developing hiring pools from the places where the talent is. This will cause students to graduate with a much larger amount of debt for a piece of paper whose value is nearly non-existent.

If the student loan default rate reaches numbers too high, then I think Americans will have a very serious conversation about whether we should put a plan in place to forgive student debt and restrict student loan funding to stop this from happening again. This is the point when even well-known public universities could go bankrupt and must restructure. Perhaps the state would save specific parts of the university like the sports teams or research programs. It's hard to say what will happen, but this could very well be comparable to the government bailing out the banks in 2008.

The Education Revelation

There are two main components, strategy and execution, when trying to accomplish any goal in life. You need to have both the correct strategy and solid execution of that strategy to be successful. For weightlifting, I've seen countless people constantly going to the gym and executing their strategy but seeing no progress. This was because they were executing a bad strategy. I've also seen people with a great muscle-building strategy, yet they make no progress. This is because they didn't put in the work to execute on their strategy. You now have The Lean Career to serve as your complete strategy for starting a great career, and it is your job to execute this strategy until you are successful. At the start, it will take time and seem like an uphill battle. You must push through, and you will come out a winner. People will try to stop you and convince you just to conform and go to college. Stand your ground.

Most people are still being indoctrinated with the lies that have been spread by corruption within the system. Now that you know the truth, it is your duty to use the wisdom distilled in this book to help others. Educate the uninformed, confused, and scared people desperately searching to find their way in life. Show them they don't have to give up years of their life and decades of debt to find success. It is up to you to help build the future. This is the education revelation.

CourseCareers

How can my company help you start your career? We help you execute the lean career strategy. If you want to use this model to start your career, then CourseCareers can serve as one of your biggest assets. We help you identify a career and learn the MVK in the most effective manner possible. We then help get you connected directly to companies looking to hire year-round interns in your specialization. Check out CourseCareers.com to see which career specializations we support as we plan to expand into many different occupations.

I suggest you sign up for our blog on CourseCareers.com to get regular guides and tips to help you start your career. We also have a tool where you can create your own education profile, which can be seen through a google search and shared with employers. Create your free profile by signing up on CourseCareers.com. Here is an example of what your profile will look like. https://coursecareers.com/profile/troy-buckholdt

My vision is to build an affordable platform that anyone can use to effectively learn the Minimum Viable Knowledge required to start their career in a wide range of occupations. Every type of job which is best learned online will eventually be supported by CourseCareers. We will also have the largest network of employers looking to hire entry-level students in these occupations.

Acknowledgements

Christy Buckholdt for supporting me through all my endeavors with this book being no exception.

Bill Epperson for teaching me to question everything I thought I knew.

Paul Terlemezian for giving me guidance on how to solve problems even before I could conceptualize the problem I was trying to solve.

Doug Mcmahon for helping guide me through the creation of this book.

All the students and parents searching for something better for giving me a reason to push through the difficulties of writing this book.

About the Author

Troy Buckholdt is an entrepreneur in the making focused on solving many of the challenges people face with higher education. He is an accomplished hitchhiker, bodybuilder, and salesman. He is a business enthusiast with his company, CourseCareers being his lifeline for fixing higher education. This company's success is his primary focus. He currently resides in Atlanta, GA.

Made in the USA
Monee, IL
28 September 2023

43635222R00104